DATE DUE

DEMCO 38-297

What People are saying about
Viatical Settlements: An Investor's Guide

This is a "must-read" for potential investors in viatical settlements and those who advise them.
— Gerry H. Goldsholle, Esq., Pres. and CEO (retired) MetLife Brokerage and Marketing Corp., former chair of American Bar Assoc. and California State Bar Insurance Committees

A shot across the bow for potential viatical investors, **Viatical Settlements: An Investor's Guide** illuminates the mysteries and minefields of viatical investing. Gloria Wolk draws on her substantial experience in the viatical settlement industry to offer a view from the trenches that all potential investors and investment advisors should read before investing a single nickel.
— Russell J. Herron, Esq., D'Ancona & Pflaum, Chicago, Ill., former executive editor, *University of Michigan Journal of Law Reform*

Truly a great job (A+). Even though viaticals have been available for a few years now, few people have heard of them. **Viatical Settlements** is easy to understand, informative, and a "must-read" for anyone considering buying or marketing viatical settlements. If this book is not on the top sellers' list it may be because it's ahead of its time.
— Blair Dean, Ph.D., stockbroker

. . . excellent research which clearly exposes the scams and risks associated with viatical investments.
— Arshad H. Khan, author (with Vaqav Zuberi) *Stock Investing for Everyone*

Everyone with vulnerable parents or friends should read this book. We didn't, and our parents were conned into several viatical investments that cost them many thousands of dollars as well as many sleepless nights.
— Richard D. Hausten, data processing manager

When I embarked on starting a viatical business to sell to investors, I naively assumed that all I would have to do is get companies to provide me with policies. After reading both of Gloria Wolk's books I am aware that the viatical industry has to be approached with open eyes, due diligence, and both of these viatical books.
— Frank Meyers, insurance agent, 12 Step Agency, Inc., Guardian Title

Wolk wrote **Cash for the Final Days: A Financial Guide for the Terminally Ill and their Advisors,** the first book to discuss viatical settlements. She now turns her attention to those who might consider buying such insurance policies.
— American Library Association *Booklist*

Viatical Settlements is a "must-read" for anyone considering investing in viaticals, who wants to protect their assets.
— Lee R. Phillips, author, *Protecting Your Financial Future*

For updated information and reviews visit our web site
http://www.viatical-expert.net

VIATICAL SETTLEMENTS

AN INVESTOR'S GUIDE

by

GLORIA GRENING WOLK, M.S.W.

*B*ialkin
ooks

Laguna Hills, CA

The author and publisher have extensively researched all sources to ensure the accuracy and completeness of information contained in this book, and assume no responsibiltiy for errors, inaccuracies, omissions, or any other inconsistency herein.

Warning—Disclaimer
We do not endorse any viatical company. Those cited in the text are for comparison purposes only. Additionally, laws change with great frequency. Readers are advised to consult an attorney, tax advisor, and/or financial planner for application to their individual situtions. For informational updates see our website at www.viatical-expert.net, or send a stamped, self-addressed envelope (first class postage) in care of the publisher.

Publisher's Cataloging-in-Publication
(Prepared by Quality Books, Inc.)

Wolk, Gloria Grening.
 Viatical settlements : an investor's guide / by Gloria Grening Wolk. — 1st ed.
 p. cm.
 Includes index.
 Preassigned LCCN: 97-97203
 ISBN: 0-9652615-7-3 (hardcover)

 1. Viatical settlements—United States. 2. Long-term care of the sick—United States—Finance. 3. Terminal care—United States—Finance. I. Title.

HG8819.W65   368.36
          QBI98-321

00 99 98 ♦ 5 4 3 2 1

Cover Design: Laurel Graphx, Vero Beach, Florida
Copy Editors: PeopleSpeak, Laguna Hills, California

Acknowledgments

A book such as this, where much of the information is new and never before published, would not be possible without the assistance and cooperation of a number of people scattered throughout North America.

For regulatory information I am indebted to Gary Thompson, Legislative Information Office of Iowa's General Assembly; Grace-Ellen McCrann, Librarian for the North Carolina Department of Cultural Resources; Andrea Leeman of the State Corporate Commission in Virginia; Pamela Beach of Michigan's Department of Consumer and Industry Services; Linda Joines of the Life/Health Group at the Texas Department of Insurance; Pamela Wood, Administrative Assistant to Attorney General Robert A. Butterworth of Florida; Mark Boozell, Director, Illinois Department of Insurance; William Kirby of Washington's Office of Insurance; John Ellis of Missouri Division of Securities; and Imants Abols of the Ontario Securities Commission for essential information about the OSCB's treatment of viatical investments.

Principals of legitimate licensed viatical settlement companies provided much valuable information as well as leads to sources of more information. Thanks to Ramon Vincente and Aaron Kokol of Viatical Benefactors (Independent Benefits); David-Irwin Bintner of AMG (Neuma); Meir Eliav of Legacy Capital (Legacy Benefits); Peggy Wallace and James Karlack of ALI (Affirmative Lifestyles); and W. Scott Page of LifeLine (Page and Associates).

Special thanks to Robert Shear, president of the Viatical Association of America and the funding company, Accelerated Benefits Capital, for allowing use of his company's underwriting guidelines for group insurance.

Special mention is due Caitlin Smith, Esq., of California's Department of Insurance, for her concern and sincere efforts to protect viators.

Contributors

Carole Fiedler, a licensed viatical broker, entered the viatical industry in 1992. An activist for the viatical industry and consumers, she has testified before the California State Senate Insurance Committee and the California State Assembly Insurance Committee on legislation, authored numerous articles, and appeared on radio and television. Web site: www.viaticalbroker.com.
Contact: Fiedler Financial Viatical Brokerage 3030 Bridgeway, Ste. 230, Sausalito, California 94965. (415) 332-1444; (800) 905-0114.

Per Larson, a New York-based financial planner and author of *Gay Money* (Simon & Schuster, 1977) has assisted more than 200 terminally ill people with negotiations for sale of their policies. Larson is a prolific writer on issues related to disability financial planning and viatical settlements. Copies of articles are available on his Web site: www.gaymoney.com.
Contact: Merrill & Mineral Springs Rd., Highland Hills, NY 10930. (914) 534-9644.

Philip Loy is president of American Viatical Services, the first nation-wide firm to specialize in life expectancy estimates and tracking of viators. Founded in 1994 to serve the viatical industry, AVS' professional staff includes physicians and scientists from the Centers for Disease Control and the National Institutes of Health.
Contact: American Viatical Service, 10896 Crabapple Road, Ste. 203, Roswell, Georgia, 30075. (770) 643-9036.

Contributors

Robert Shear, current president of the Viatical Association of America and founder and CEO of funding firm Accelerated Benefits Capital, brought to the viatical indsutry a background in securities and real estate syndication. He is responsible for directing the company's activities, setting underwriting criteria, developing risk management procedures, financing and creating the systems used to monitor the portfolio. Contact: 25900 Greenfield Rd., Ste. 230, Oak Park, Michigan, 48237. (248) 967-4400.

Jack W. Traylor, D.P.A., is president of T&T Reports, Inc., a consulting company that issues insurance company solvency reports. Currently a Certified Insurance Receiver, he is former Deputy Director, Florida Department of Insurance; Chief Operating Officer, Office of the Special Deputy Receiver, Illinois Department of Insurance; and Bureau Chief, Rehabilitation and Liquidating, Florida Department of Insurance.
Web site: www.godby.leon.k12.fl.us/~godbyweb/tt/index.html
Contact: T&T Reports, P.O. Box 3429, Tallahassee, Florida, 32315-3429. (850) 402-0250.

David E. Wood, Esq., managing partner of the law firm of Wood and Associates, LLP, represents insurance industry clients throughout North America in matters related to insurance coverage and business fraud. Former partner and department chair with a multinational insurance defense firm, he is a member of the Tort and Insurance Practice Section of the American Bar Association, and has spoken at conferences and seminars hosted by the ABA National Institute, the California Bankers Association, and the Independent Agents Association. Web site: www.wood-associates.com.
Contact: Wood & Associates, LLP, 751 Daily Drive, Ste. 250, Camarillo, California, 93010. (805) 484-3940

CONTENTS

Contents

In Memory of Viktor Frankl

1905 - 1997

INTRODUCTION:
WHO THIS BOOK IS FOR

Y OU'RE AN INDIVIDUAL INVESTOR LOOKING FOR HIGHER YIELDS, OR an investment advisor whose clients are individuals, a homeowner's association, a church group, or a pension fund. You heard about viatical settlement investments on the radio or television, or a newspaper advertisement, or on the Internet. If you're a financial professional it's likely you were solicited directly—through trade magazines, the mail, and seminars. Regardless of which avenue the information traveled, you probably heard/read something like this:[a]

- ♦ "The Biggest, Little-Known High Yield, Safe Money Investment"
- ♦ "Profits guaranteed"
- ♦ "Your principal is 100% guaranteed"
- ♦ "Earn 15% - 25% On Your Money With No Market Risk and No Speculation"
- ♦ Contractually Guaranteed 42% return on capital"

No doubt you tried to learn more. You searched for unbiased, objective information and discovered, instead, that few people ever heard about viatical settlements. One reason is that viatical settlements are a relatively new industry

---

[a] Throughout the text you will find quotes from viatical companies. These are quoted exactly, without corrections to punctuation or grammar.

and, until recently, a private industry.[a]

The viatical industry was begun by wealthy investors who were backed by hefty bank credit lines. These investors formed companies known as *viatical funding firms.*[b] Then other viatical companies formed—viatical brokerages. Viatical brokers are similar to real estate brokers in that they assist sellers to find a buyer and negotiate a price.

In 1996, 11 years after the viatical industry began in the U.S., the scene changed dramatically. Dozens of new companies rushed into the arena. Many of them are maverick companies that operate in defiance of state viatical laws. Others are nothing more than marketing companies. Marketing companies do not buy life insurance polices. In fact, it takes little capital to start a marketing company and there is little risk: They do not invest their own dollars. Their profits come from skimming fees from the top of investors' purchase funds. This, of course, leaves less money for patients who sell their policies.

Some wary investors who wanted to buy viatical contracts didn't want to deal with these johnny-come-lately companies. They phoned established, licensed viatical providers to ask if policies were available to individual investors. In this way demand created supply: Legitimate funding firms decided to offer viatical investments to the public.

Promotional campaigns are hot and heavy and, with rare exceptions, target Middle America. Viatical companies seek sizable investments—sums in the five figures. Since the folks of Middle America rarely have large sums to invest, viatical companies urge these investors to convert their CDs (Certificates of Deposit) and IRAs (Individual Retirement Accounts) into viaticals investments.

When seniors are the target, the favorite ploy of sales promoters is to tout the safety of viaticals—by comparing them to CDs or annuities. A different

---

[a] The word viatical is from the Latin *viaticum* which means *provisions for a journey.* Policy owners who sell their death benefits are known as *viators.*

[b] Funding firms buy directly from sellers, and usually invest for their own portfolios.

approach is used with socially conscious investors, the type of person who shuns investments in alcohol and tobacco:

> For those of you with a heart of compassion, participating in this unique program goes beyond the everyday investment. Your rewards are both humanitarian and Financial.[a] [sic]

When viatical companies extol the humanitarian aspect of this investment, their motive is not to appeal to someone's good heart. Rather, they use this sales pitch to overcome the squeamishness of people who consider investing in someone's death as "ghoulish," or who view this as an investment in "Death Futures."

Despite the manipulations of sales promoters, these truly are humanitarian investments. The viatical industry provides cash to desperately ill people at a time when illness has robbed them of their earning ability, and medical expenses rob them of their savings.

Viatical settlements are used to buy medical care many health plans don't pay for, such as expensive painkilling medicines, organ transplants, or items as mundane and inexpensive as bottled water.[b] These funds may prevent foreclosure of the family home; or help a family acquire a specially-built van to transport a wheel-chair bound patient. Sometimes viatical settlements are used for a last, great vacation; or a child or grandchild's wedding; or to enroll a child at college now, rather than postpone college for lack of financing.[c] In one way or another, viatical settlements enhance the quality of life for people with limited life expectancies and for everyone dear to them.

Although viatical settlements make a major difference in the quality of life

---

[a] From the Internet web site of a Colorado-based company.

[b] Bottled water is a necessity for people who have compromised immune systems, a frequent occurrence for patients with cancer, AIDS, or ALS (Lou Gehrig's Disease).

[c] Viator refers to the seller of a life insurance policy.

for patients and their families, the humanitarian aspect is turned into a high pressure sales tool when a cautious investor hesitates to write out a check.

> If you are uncomfortable with the idea of offering others a `living alternative' to terminal illness, we would strongly suggest that you take your financial investment elsewhere . . . as we are a company that is entirely about people.[a]

Pressure tactics are unnecessary. Profits *are* possible. As with any investment, profits may be modest or they may be astronomical. As with any investment, there are risks. In this case, the risks are far more than most investors are told. This is the primary purpose of this book: to protect investors.

Since little is known about viatical investments and even less about the risks, some of what you're about to learn may scare the dickens out of you: con artists, Ponzi schemes, insurance policies that won't pay a nickel, and terminally ill people with their own get-rich-quick schemes. It's possible to avoid the scams, but it's not possible to avoid the misinformation spread by most viatical companies. Here are a few samples:

◆ Medical: *An AIDS patient who takes "the cocktail" has only a year to live.*

This statement reassures those who know nothing about AIDS (Acquired Immune Deficiency Syndrome), who search the medical records to find the word "cocktail."

◆ Tax: *The proceeds of a life insurance policy are tax-free.*

"Even to investors?" you may ask.

"Yes, even to investors," you'll be told.

◆ Another tax claim: *Approved for IRAs.*

Approved by whom? The IRS (Internal Revenue Service) does not approve specific investments.

------

[a] From the Internet Web site of a West Palm Beach, Florida company.

♦ Insurance: *No life insurance company ever failed to pay a death claim.*

This is blatantly untrue.

Then there are claims that investors can double their money in a year; claims of 70 percent and higher yields; claims of stockbrokers leaving Wall Street to concentrate on this new, powerful investment. People believe these claims and turn over their entire savings to total strangers. Many investors are naive but others who should know better—homeowners' associations and pension funds, which have professional advisors—are investing in viaticals. Church groups are investing. Banks are selling them, and repeating the same misinformation to bank investors.

If investors are uninformed, the odds are they will lose money. Whether you're an individual investor or an investment advisor, **Viatical Settlements: An Investor's Guide** will give you the tools to perform due diligence. Due diligence is

The prudence and effort that is ordinarily used by a reasonable person under the circumstances.[1]

In other words, due diligence requires caution, inspection, study, meticulousness. Only after you have exercised due diligence can you can make an informed decision about investing. If you decide to invest or advise clients to invest, the information in this book will help you take control of the investment process to assure greater protection than currently exists.

Individual investors may find the task of due diligence to be daunting. As an alternative, leave the nitty-gritty of due diligence to investment advisors and use this book to prepare you to evaluate advisors. The person you choose to help you should be a licensed or registered financial professional capable of advising you about mutual funds, annuities, stocks and bonds as well as viaticals.

Before you set out to interview financial professionals, draw up a list of questions based on the information in this book. If you find yourself in a room with someone who doesn't know as much as you do about the risks, or who hasn't the personal wherewithal to demand that viatical companies make contractual changes, go to another advisor.[2]

Investment advisors need this book because, unless they perform due diligence, they may recommend viaticals to clients for whom this investment is inappropriate. If you fail to perform due diligence and if you don't demand contractual changes to safeguard your clients' investments, your clients are likely to lose money. If that happens, you may find your license and your career at risk.

Conversely, if investment advisors are diligent and also demand that viatical companies make changes to protect their clients, they can help clean up this industry and assure its longevity. Which brings us to the second purpose of this book: to protect the existence of the legitimate viatical industry.

Although the viatical industry is exploding all over the map, it is at risk. Investors have lost hundreds of millions of dollars due to undisclosed risks, misinformation, and little or no regulation. If this continues, eventually the money supply will dry up. Then the industry will collapse. If the industry collapses, everyone loses—you, me, friends, relatives—whoever may one day be desperately ill and financially desperate.

If investors learn how to avoid the risks and how to mitigate risks that are unavoidable, there will be profits for everyone—investors, viators, and viatical companies. This *is* possible.

Most risks are avoidable—with knowledge.

1. William P. Statsky, *West's' Legal Thesaurus/Dictionary*. West Publishing Company, St. Paul, 1985.

2. The Investment Advisors Act of 1940 "does not provide any guarantee of competence on the part of advisors; it only helps to protect the investor against fraudulent and unethical practices by the advisor." Lawrence J. Gitman and Michael D. Joehnk, *Fundamentals of Investing*, Second Edition. Harper & Row, New York, 1984.

CHAPTER ONE

❧

OVERVIEW

> In the mid 1980s Robert Worley, Jr., a New Mexico-based
> financial planner, gathered a group of investors to fund the
> purchase of a terminally ill client's life insurance. These
> people formed *Living Benefits*, the first viatical settlement
> company in North America.

I NVESTORS ARE BUYING LIFE INSURANCE, BUT MAKE NO MISTAKE: THIS
is an investment. Investors buy low (a discounted death benefit) and, if
all goes well, collect high: full death benefits when the insured dies.

DISCOUNTED PURCHASE PRICE

Viatical companies calculate profits on the difference between purchase price
and full death benefits. For example, a policy with a face amount of $100,000

may have a purchase price ranging from $50,000 to $80,000.[a]

This steep discount is the reason viaticals have potential to be very profitable. But not always. Like the old rhyme about the little girl with a little curl: When they're good, they're very good, and when they're bad, they're horrid.

RISKS

When viatical investments are "horrid" it's due to undisclosed risks, some of which can lead to loss of the entire investment. Three academics who collaborated on an article for the Journal of Certified Life Underwriters suggest limiting purchases to contracts with the following characteristics:

- ♦ insured has a life expectancy of three years or less;
- ♦ life insurer has a Best's rating of A or better;
- ♦ policy has been in force beyond the contestability period;
- ♦ policy has a waiver of premium provision;
- ♦ coverage must be assignable, and the investor must be able to be named the beneficiary;
- ♦ viator must be legally sane;
- ♦ suicide exclusion time period has passed;
- ♦ if viator is still working and sells group policy, then he or she must be able to maintain the face value of the policy after he/she quits working;
- ♦ if a group policy, the master contract must allow continued coverage even if the master contract is terminated.[1]

This formula offers minimal protection for investors, as you soon will learn. Nearly every item on the list is far more complicated than these authors acknowledge. Nearly every item can leave investors exposed to serious risks.

Why don't viatical companies disclose the risks? There is no requirement for them to do so. Then again, few viatical companies know all the risks—and this includes those companies that invest their own money.

The risk most frequently mentioned is "maturity risk," a term coined by the viatical industry. Maturity risk refers to the possibility that viators will live

---

[a] *Face amount* and *face value* are used interchangeably for death benefit.

years longer than estimated life expectancy. Investors are told that if a viator lives six years instead of two, yield may drop to 6 percent—the equivalent of a CD—and "that's not terribly bad."

When sales promoters reveal mortality risk it's a tongue-in-cheek disclosure, like tossing a bone to a dog to keep the dog from chasing rabbits. But investors need to go after rabbits. Investors need to know all the risks, particularly those that could wipe out their entire investment. For example:

The investor buys a death benefit at 80 percent of face value for a policy that insures a patient with a life expectancy estimated at one year. The patient lives 5 years, perhaps ten years. With each passing year, the yield drops. By the time the policy "matures," the yield is zero.

Then zero yield turns into loss: the viator outlives life expectancy by several years *and* investors must pay premiums to prevent the policy from lapsing.

Whether this happens depends in part on the expertise of medical consultants. Equally important are the methods used to estimate life expectancy.[a] Philip Loy describes these methods as well as health conditions where life expectancy cannot be predicted in chapter 6, "Predicting Life Expectancy." [b]

What if the insurer goes "belly-up"? No problem, investors are told: death claims will be paid by state guarantee funds. Case closed? Not according to Jack Traylor (chapter 7, "Belly-up Insurance"), whose expertise was honed assisting state insurance departments with resolution of insurer insolvencies.

What about "maverick" companies—those that operate without licenses? Per Larson has a few warnings about mavericks (see appendix VI).

What if the viator lied on the insurance application by not disclosing a serious health condition? No problem, investors are told, since we buy policies

---

[a] This assumes that the viatical company prices the policy accurately.

[b] It also depends on whether the viatical company tells investors the truth about life expectancy. Some sell 48 months as 12 months. See chapter 6 and appendix VII.

that are past the contestability period. That means insurers can't contest the policy. Case closed? Not according to David Wood, a litigation attorney who specializes in insurance law (chapter 9: "Viators and Fraud: A Wake-up Call for Investors").

What happens if you buy a policy from an insured, but the entire sale is prohibited by local law? See chapter 8, "Fraud Watch."

If investors are to avoid these risks, they need to know what to look for *before* signing a check. Once they invest, risk avoidance is the option of the viatical company. And this is the crux of the problem: *Investors are totally dependent on the viatical company.*

It's the viatical company that selects the viator; evaluates life expectancy; verifies insurance coverage; sets the purchase price; negotiates with the viator; and performs essential after-sale functions—without which investors might lose every dollar invested.

What you're about to learn will alert you to these risks and help prevent loss of principal due to undisclosed as well as identified risks.

SCAMS APLENTY

The majority of companies that offer viatical settlement contracts are not legitimate. For every legitimate company that currently markets to the public, there are dozens of maverick companies with scant knowledge about viatical settlements. These companies, the "underbelly" of the industry, may be difficult to distinguish from legitimate companies since they use much the same language and concepts. However, they don't practice what they preach—as you will learn in the following pages.

Far worse than the mavericks are the con artists. Viatical cons were sprung as early as 1985—the very year of the founding of the first funding firm in the U.S.[2]

That year the National Association of Securities Administrators Association (NASAA), a regulatory body, issued a public warning about viatical hoaxes that promised "big returns to investors who bought life insurance from AIDS patients who rarely existed."[3]

The companies alleged to be engaged in these frauds were National Insurance Marketing, Inc., of Panama City, Florida; and Life Partners, Inc., of Waco, Texas. At the time neither of these companies was brought up on charges, and National Insurance Marketing seems to have disappeared, or the principals recycled themselves with another name and similar company (which frequently happens). Life Partners, however, remains to this day a prominent if controversial player in the viatical settlement business. More about Life Partners later.

It was not long afterward that United Benefits Corporation of Boca Raton, Florida, came on the scene. United Benefits became notorious within the viatical industry. This company never bought a single life insurance policy. Instead, investors' funds—between $3.5 million and $4.5 million—paid for luxuries for the principals of the company.[4] Bad as this was, it pales in comparison to the one perpetrated nearly ten years later by Personal Choice Opportunities. More on this in chapter 8, "Fraud Watch."

THE LEGITIMATE INDUSTRY

These stories are not meant to scare you off. Quite the opposite. Since the purpose of this book is to help you invest safely, these stories are intended to underscore the value of doing your homework.

How does one go about investing safely in viatical contracts? First, learn about the viatical process, especially how life expectancy is predicted since this is what you're buying: a *prediction*.

Equally important, investors need to know about life insurance. You don't need to know every tedious detail but you should be aware of those aspects that relate to investment risk.

Once you are aware of the risks, you need to consider how viatical settlements compare with other investments. Does this investment meet your goals, both short-term and long-term? Is it appropriate for you?

Finally, if you decide to invest, you need to know how to choose a viatical company—one that is *legitimate*. Chapter 4 includes criteria to help you evaluate the legitimacy of viatical company. Then you must scour the contracts of these companies, to be assured that you are not exposed to undue risks. Before you close this book you will know which changes to the contract are necessary to protect your investment, and the best way to go about demanding these changes.

END NOTES

1. David W. Sommer, Ph.D., Sandra G. Gustavson, Ph.D., CEBS, James S. Trieschmann, DA, CLU, CPCU. "Viatical Settlements: Perspectives of Investors, Regulators, and Insureds." Journal of Chartered Life Underwriters, January 1997. Available: http://iix.com/clu/journal/J0397A4.htm.
Somer is an assistant professor of risk management and insurance at the University of Georgia; Gustavson is the Bradford McFadden Professor of Personal Financial Management at the University of Georgia, where she heads the Risk Management and Insurance Progam. Trieschmann is associate dean of the Terry College of Business at the University of Georgia and past president of the American Risk and Insurance Association.

2. Viatical settlements occurred in private transactions in Europe before it became a formal industry in the United States.

3. *Wall Street Journal,* August 20, 1992; *Jet,* September 7, 1992.

4. A widely-publicized case. The summary that appears in the text is taken from a news release, *"Viatical Settlements—Humanitarian Investments with Great Risk of Fraud,"* May 2, 1996, published by the Office of the Comptroller for the State of Florida. Available: http://www.dbf.state.fl.us/alert5.html.

CHAPTER TWO

❖

SALES PITCHES

Anyone can sell this investment. Sales agents are likely to
tell investors anything that persuades them to write a check.
Here's a sampling of those claims, and the truth behind
them.

THE REASON ANYONE CAN SELL VIATICAL CONTRACTS TO INVESTORS
is that no federal securities law applies here. Although fraud and
misrepresentation laws apply, they are applied retroactively. There is no law
that protects investors before they write that five-figure check.

Currently there are no licensing requirements for sales agents, no
educational requirements, and no requirements for disclosure of finances or
felony convictions.

You may have heard mention of viatical regulation. These regulations are
enacted by the individual states and have nothing to do with viatical

investments. Where viatical regulation exists—in less than half the states—it's designed solely to protect terminally ill sellers (viators). At this writing only one state has any provision to protect viatical investors.[a]

After an individual solicited more than $700,000 from senior citizens, Louisiana amended its viatical settlement law

> **to include under insurance department regulations an individual who solicited funding.**[1]

This is minimal protection and probably not highly effective. Instead, an increasing number of states now consider viatical sales made to multiple owners (i.e., "fractionalized shares") to be securities.[2] Since this is not true of all states, investors and investment advisors should check with the state agency in charge of securities to determine if viatical investments must be registered as a security, and the sales agent licensed to sell securities. That's all you will learn. Don't expect that agency to provide other information or advice about this investment. If you seek sound, objective advice, you will have to rely on other resources.

It's likely that your favorite financial advisor will greet questions about viatical settlements with a blank stare. Most attorneys, accountants, stockbrokers, and other financial advisors know little about viatical settlements—unless they're part of a viatical marketing group (and then they won't stop talking).

Nor will you learn much truth from viatical salespeople. Viatical companies prefer to recruit insurance agents and financial planners, but the majority of viatical salespeople are hired through employment ads for "aggressive sales/marketing professionals." When you ask questions, they will parrot what they were taught—if they learned it correctly. One sales agent, for example, said that the buyer/investor is called a viator. She didn't know that

---

[a] As of June 1998 Florida's viatical regulations will carry an amendment that requires certain disclosures to investors. This is minimal protection, since it is difficult to enforce.

buyers are buyers and *sellers* are viators.

Another viatical sales person, Mal—you'll hear more about him later —repeatedly referred to the viatical company as "The Insurer." When asked if insurance companies were involved in viaticals, he corrected himself, then made the same mistake later on.

These stories may seem trivial, but sales agents' statements often are pivotal in the decision-making process. Since little is known about viatical settlements, most investors and a good portion of sophisticated investment advisors believe whatever they are told.[a]

Here are some of the claims repeated by most viatical companies, followed by the truth behind these statements.[b]

ANY AIDS PATIENT WHO TAKES THE "3-DRUG COCKTAIL" HAS 12 MONTHS TO LIVE.

False. About one third of AIDS patients do very well on the "3-drug cocktail."[3] The following is quoted from Donna Fleming, director of social services at AIDS Services Foundation (ASF):

> With more than 40% of our clients now having a CD4 count over 200 and many considering returning to work, a AIDS diagnosis is not an accurate indicator of the health or needs of clients.[4]

Fleming went on to say, "There are . . . many with an AIDS diagnosis who are working."

Whether patients do well depends on several factors: their health before beginning the regimen, their compliance—how faithfully they follow the strict

---

[a] In May, 1998, The Securities and Exchange Commission (SEC) accused one of the largest viatical firms of selling unregistered settlements and misleading investors about their rate of return. For details, see chapter 8, "Fraud Watch."

[b] These ads are direct quotes but sources are omitted, since many viatical companies use the same words to make the same claims.

schedule, and their tolerance for the drugs.

Some AIDS patients can't tolerate protease inhibitors—the essence of the 3-drug combination. They have great difficulty with side effects, become sicker, and have to discontinue taking the drugs. Most switch from one protease inhibitor to another, and an alternative may work. Or not.

The point is, don't fall for a sales pitch based on the mortality of AIDS patients. See chapter 6, "Predicting Life Expectancy."

INVESTORS CAN GET THE INSURANCE PROCEEDS TAX FREE, SINCE LIFE INSURANCE BENEFITS ARE TAX FREE.

False. Proceeds are tax-free when paid in the traditional manner. The "traditional manner" is when the named beneficiary has an *insurable interest*. Insurable interest means the beneficiary suffers loss if the insured dies. These beneficiaries may be loved ones, friends, business partners, but not investors. Investors don't suffer loss when a viator dies.[5]

Additionally, when a policy is transferred (sold) for value, tax-free status flies out the window. Transfer for value converts the life insurance policy into an investment for the new owner—a taxable investment.[a]

If the buyer/investor happens to be a relative who has an insurable interest, proceeds of the viatical investment will be taxable nonetheless. When there is transfer for value, insurable interest doesn't matter.[6]

INVESTORS CAN GET INSURANCE PROCEEDS TAX FREE, SINCE THERE'S NO REPORTING TO IRS.

True. At this time, insurance companies don't send out form 1099 when they pay death benefits. The reason is that normally, death benefits paid to named beneficiaries are tax-free. That is not to say that insurers never send out 1099s in connection with life insurance proceeds. They do—when they pay interest on the death benefit.[7]

---

[a] Transfer for value means money is exchanged.

But this is this message from many viatical companies:

Viatical investors pay taxes voluntarily.

Should you "volunteer" to pay the tax? Keep this in mind: There is no statute of limitations on tax fraud. You may escape this tangled web for years—and get caught when you're deep into retirement. Then, if you're found guilty of tax fraud, you'll owe huge interest and penalties.

NO LIFE INSURANCE COMPANY EVER FAILED TO PAY A DEATH CLAIM.
False. For details, see chapters 8 and 9.

IRA QUALIFIED.
False. Variations of this claim include "Approved for IRAs," and "Suitable for IRAs." The facts are these: the Internal Revenue Service does not approve specific investments. Equally important, life insurance as an IRA investment has been a "prohibited transaction" for many years, according to Internal Revenue Code (IRC) § 408(a)(3)25.

Despite this prohibition, you'll hear that Life Partners and its clones concocted a way around the law.[a] Their method is to have the IRA lend money to a trust. Then the trust invests in viatical contracts.

Rather than find a way around the law, these companies simply substitute one violation for another. *Loans from IRAs are prohibited by law.* Life Partners may have gotten away with this scheme so far, but that doesn't make it legal.[8]

Once the IRS catches on to this, the amount of the IRA loan will be immediately taxable as a distribution. Then investors may have to pay the 10 percent additional tax on premature distributions, and the 15 percent tax on

---

[a] Life Partners is the viatical firm that was brought to federal court by the Securities and Exchange Commission (SEC), a federal regulatory and enforcement agency. For details, see Wolk, "Cash for the Final Days: A Financial Guide for the Terminally Ill and their Advisors," chapter 6.

excess distributions. More about IRAs in chapters 4, "Contracts Compared," and 10, "Wealthy or Wannabe?"

STATE VIATICAL LAWS VERIFY THAT THIS INVESTMENT IS FOR REAL AND REGULATED.
False. State viatical laws don't address the investment aspects of viaticals. Since they don't regulate viatical investments, they don't verify a single thing about this investment—not even that it's "real."

THE LICENSING PROCESS MEANS THAT A VIATICAL COMPANY HAD TO GO THROUGH THE SCRUTINY OF AN AUDIT BY THE STATE THEY ARE LICENSED IN.
False. None of the states requires an audit in order to apply for a viatical license. Rather, some states require license applicants to provide audited financial statements. This means that instead of using do-it-yourself software, applicants must pay a certified public accountant (CPA) to prepare the documents.

Note: Audited financial statements are not necessarily accurate. The biggest and best accounting firms have been duped. Furthermore, accounting firms do not guarantee their statements.

IF A VIATICAL COMPANY SURVIVED A STATE'S TOUGH LICENSING PROCESS, IT'S A VERY GOOD SIGN.
False. No state has a tough licensing process. At its worst, the licensing process is laborious and might lead to a migraine—like preparing your tax return. This is not true of all states. In some states, it's less difficult to get licensed than to bake cookies. Viatical companies simply register and pay a token fee. This has the effect of saying, "Our company is now here in Texas, trying to make some money in the viatical business."

There are two major problems with licensing: Compliance and enforcement. Regarding compliance, the process fails to weed out illegal companies. Illegals don't bother to apply for a viatical license. Regarding enforcement, most states don't supervise the activities of the companies. They wait for a written consumer complaint.

One thing that irks licensed viatical firms is that some states prohibit resales of these policies to any but another viatical provider licensed in that state. This reduces the liquidity—resale value—of viatical investments.[9, 10]

If you buy a policy sold by a viator from a state that prohibits such sales, the transaction could be voided by a court. This means you could lose your entire investment. For details, see chapter 8.

THE BEST LICENSE FOR A VIATICAL SALES PERSON TO HAVE IS A LIFE INSURANCE LICENSE. NEXT WOULD BE A VIATICAL BROKER LICENSE.

False. Although life insurance agents must pass a state licensing examination and many states require continuing education courses, most life insurance agents have little knowledge about viatical settlements or, for that matter, insurers' Accelerated Death Benefits.

Viatical brokers, who assist terminally ill people with the sale of their policies, do not have to meet stringent requirements. In actual fact, there are no standards: Brokers just file some papers and pay a fee. In California, Senate Bill 1623 would have allowed insurance agents and brokers to become viatical brokers simply by deciding they wanted to do this. If the insurance commissioner later discovered these agents were guilty of sins of omission or commission, they would be banned from viatical transactions but suffer no repercussions to their insurance license.[a]

NOT ONE STATE REQUIRES A SECURITIES LICENSE TO SELL VIATICAL CONTRACTS.

True. Viatical investments are not securities. Anyone can legally sell a single policy to an investor.

---

[a] In response to opposition, this provision of SB 1623 was withdrawn on May 14, 1998.

However, this is not necessarily true for co-ownership, or "fractionalized shares" of viatical insurance policies. In some states fractionalized shares are considered to be securities and viatical sales people must be registered.

THE SUPREME COURT HAS RULED VIATICAL SETTLEMENTS TO BE A SAFE INVESTMENT, AND UNNECESSARY FOR SEC REGULATION.
False. At this writing, the U.S. Supreme Court has not addressed viatical settlements in any way or form. Nor has any state supreme court addressed this issue. There was one federal court case, but it had nothing to do with the question of viaticals as safe investments.[11]

OWNERSHIP OF THE POLICY IS TAKEN OVER BY THE ESCROW COMPANY, AS A SAFETY MEASURE.
False. Neither the escrow company nor the viatical company should own your property; many problems may result. For example, what would happen if the company that owned the policy went out of business? Other risks that may occur when the viatical company or its agent are owners can are detailed in chapter 5, "Finding Risk."

PREMIUM PAYMENTS ARE TAKEN OVER BY THE VIATICAL COMPANY ON BEHALF OF THE INVESTORS.
No viatical company pays premiums out of its own pocket. Premiums are paid from purchase funds. If the insured outlives life expectancy and further payments are required, these additional premiums will be paid by you, the investor. For details, see chapter 4.

INVESTING IN VIATICAL SETTLEMENT POLICIES AS AN INDIVIDUAL ALLOWS FOR A HIGHER PAYMENT TO THE PATIENT FOR THEIR INSURANCE POLICY BENEFITS.
False. Patients lose thousands of dollars with viatical settlements. If patients qualify for insurer benefits, they get much more money since insurers pay

almost dollar for dollar.[a]

The main problem with insurers' pre-death benefits is timing. Eligibility for these benefits usually is restricted to insureds with life expectancies of 6 to 12 months. If a viator needs cash at 24 or 36 months, viatical settlements may be the only answer.[b]

TERMINALLY ILL INDIVIDUALS RECEIVE AT MOST 50% OF THE DEATH BENEFIT FROM THEIR INSURER.

False. Some insurers pay as much as 98 percent or 100 percent. Although it's also true that some insurers limit payment to 50 percent of the death benefit, insureds don't lose the remaining death benefit. It's reserved for named beneficiaries.

Then there are times when viatical providers as well as insurers have no choice but to limit pre-death, or Accelerated Death Benefits, to 50 percent. Some states restrict the amount of pre-death benefits if the insured (viator) has dependent children.[c]

A related—and totally false—claim about insurance companies is that insureds must "agree to use the proceeds only for the purposes permitted by the insurance company's Accelerated Benefit Rider." There are no restrictions on how these funds are spent. Even if insurers tried to restrict how funds were spent, they would have no way to control the money was it was paid to the viator.

---

[a] Insurer benefits have a variety of names, e.g., Accelerated Death Benefits, Living Benefits, Terminal Illness Rider, etc.

[b] Some insures pay no more than 50 percent of the death benefit, but the balance can be sold to a viatical company. For details about Accelerated Death Benefits, see "Cash for the Final Days."

[c] New Hampshire requires 50 percent of death benefits be reserved for dependent children.

YOU CAN CONTACT OUR ATTORNEYS TO VERIFY THAT WE ARE A LEGITIMATE COMPANY.
Of course you can talk to their attorneys, and they'll be as friendly and reassuring as the sales agent. Especially if the attorneys are brothers-in-law to one of the principals or shareholders in the company.

NO COMMISSIONS REQUIRED.
This is what *investors* are told. But see the next claim.

THE AGENT RECEIVES A GENEROUS COMMISSION FOR FACILITATING THE TRANSACTION.
This is what *agents* are told—by the very same company as above.

WE HAD NEARLY $3 MILLION IN REVENUE LAST YEAR.
If this is important to you, ask to see audited financial statements. But the company's revenues are not significant—not if you maintain control over the policy you buy.

DURING THE MONTH OF MAY, IN EXCESS OF $10 MILLION OF INVESTOR MONEY WAS PROCESSED THROUGH OUR SYSTEM.
This is not important to investors. What's important is how the company underwrites the risks, how it prices policies, and how it monitor viators.

Then again, this could be a problem. Some viatical companies boast of millions of investors' dollars coming through their "system," but they don't have enough "inventory" of policies to place these funds. Thus, investor funds may sit idle, in escrow, for as long as 5 months.

WE PROCESS ABOUT 100 APPLICATIONS A MONTH WITH POLICIES AVERAGING $150,000.
What does this have to do with the safety of *your* money?

WE EXCEED THE REQUIREMENTS AND LAWS REGARDING VIATICAL SETTLEMENTS.

There are no requirements and *no* laws regarding viatical investments.

100% OF THE INVESTMENT IS PUT TO WORK; BUYERS INCUR NO EXPENSE IN THIS ENTIRE TRANSACTION.

False. For more information, see chapter 4, "Contracts Compared."

THE HOME OFFICE BROKERAGE MAKES A PROFIT ON THE SPREAD BETWEEN THE PURCHASE PRICE AND SELLING PRICE OF THE POLICY.

True. The company (the "home office brokerage") skims its fee off the top of the purchase price. You may pay $80,000, the viator gets $55,000, and the company pockets $25,000.

ALL RETURNS (BOTH PRINCIPAL AND PROFIT) ARE KNOWN IN ADVANCE TO THE PENNY. [sic]

True, if this refers to the dollar amount paid when the insured dies. You'll get the full death benefit if nothing is wrong with the policy and the sale itself is not illegal.

Profit, however, is another story. Profit depends on how long you wait until you are paid.

THE VIATICAL PROGRAM GUARANTEES A TOTAL FIXED RETURN ON PRINCIPAL. [sic]

False. If you paid $30,000 for the right to receive a death benefit of $50,000, you may receive $50,000 one day, but this is not the same as "return on principal" or "yield."

Yield cannot be guaranteed. It depends on the relationship between life expectancy and actual date of death. What happens to the yield if an insured outlives life expectancy and investors must pay premiums for years and years? Yes, you may get that "guaranteed" death benefit but if you financed it with extra, out-of-pocket dollars, these extra dollars lower your yield. As nationally syndicated financial journalist Jane Bryant Quinn explained,

> Take that five-year, 75 percent return. That refers to the lump sum you'll receive when the sick person eventually dies. But it doesn't tell you the annual yield. If the death occurs at the end of five years, your annual, compounded yield would be roughly 11.5 percent. [12]

This assumes, of course, that the sale is legitimate; that the insurer doesn't go out of business, and that the viator doesn't disappear (there's no payment without a death certificate). Then you'll have nothing to worry about but yield.

YIELD IS TAX DEFERRED UNTIL PAY DAY.
True. There's no tax because there's no gain to report until pay day.

YIELDS AS HIGH AS 100%
A modest brag, considering that one company boasts of 122 percent yields. Here's a sampling of other claims lifted from the marketing materials of viatical companies based at the following locations:

- Boca Raton, Florida: returns from 24 percent to 42 percent upon maturity
- Jacksonville, Florida: "guaranteed" one-year returns of 12 percent, two year returns of 28 percent, three year returns of 42 percent
- Pompano Beach, Florida: returns from 10 percent for a short-term purchase to 98 percent for a long-term purchase (with terms that range from six months to five years)
- Clearwater, Florida: "guaranteed" returns as high as 60 percent
- Tucson, Arizona: "historical" annual yields ranging from 15 to 25 percent; adding that yield can get as high as 80 to 100 percent, "depending on the life expectancy of the insured" [a]
- Holland, Michigan: "guaranteed profits of 11 to 70 percent"

---

[a] "Historical" returns in an industry with no history?

♦ Doniphan, Missouri: "25% annual interest guaranteed"

♦ Harrison, Ohio: "total fixed return of 12%, 28% or 42%"

This is how a Colorado-based firm explains "fixed" returns:

If a patient with a 36 month life expectancy actually lived 36 months (3 years), the fixed return is still 42%, but the annual return would be 14 percent (42% divided by 3 years). If the patient (Viator) died in 12 months, the actual annualized return would be 42 percent.

It's numbers like these that led Glenn Pomeroy, North Dakota's insurance commissioner, to say, "If someone's able to get that sort of return, the sick person—the person who's dying—is getting ripped off."

END NOTES

1. From the minutes of the August 22, 1997 meeting of NAIC's *Viatical Settlements Working Group of the Life Insurance (A) Committee*, Kansas City, Missouri. The meeting was attended by representatives of the insurance and viatical settlements industries, working together to revise the Viatical Settlements Model Act drafted by the National Association of Insurance Commissioners.

2. At this writing the states that consider sales of viatical contracts to multiple owners include California, Kansas, Michigan, Missouri, North Dakota, South Dakota, Virginia. Page & Associates, parent company of LifeLine, has a legal opinion from a California-licensed attorney which assures the company that viatical sales are not securities if investors are irrevocable beneficiaries who are paid directly by the insurance company. In other words, securities are defined on the basis of how death benefits are distributed: If distributed by the viatical company or its agent, it would be securities.

3. In the March 26, 1998 edition of *The Wall Street Journal* Michael Waldholz reported on research results from nine medical centers around the country: Mortality from AIDS had "declined 75% from January 1994 to June 1997."

4. AIDS Services Foundation (ASF) is located in Orange County, California. This quote is from the September/October 1997 issue of ASF's newsletter, *The Voice*.

5. Insurable interest, as defined by the California Insurance Code § 10110.1 (a) is:

> an interest based upon a reasonable expectation of pecuniary advantage through the continued life, health, or bodily safety of another person and consequent loss by reason of that person's death. . ..

6. IRC Section 101(a)(1) treats life insurance proceeds as not includable in the beneficiary's gross income for federal income tax purposes. Transfer for value is one of the exceptions to this rule. Therefore, proceeds paid to investors are taxable to the investors. See, "Tax Aspects of Life Insurance," Kenneth Black, Jr., and, Harold Skipper, Jr., in *Life Insurance*, 11th edition (Prentice-Hall, Inc., 1987).

7. Interest is paid on the death benefit if payment has been delayed for any reason. There also may be taxable interest on cash values. Moreover, taxes may be withheld if the policy owner is subject to backup withholding or estate taxes.

END NOTES

8. IRA loans to a trust did not become legal simply because neither the SEC nor the federal judges who heard this case were aware that IRA loans are prohibited. According to Gerry H. Goldsholle, Esq., a similar error was made by the appeals court when it failed to recognize that this tactic turned viaticals into securities: "Lending to a trust makes the trust the instrument. It is clearly a security, even if the underlying asset is not a security."

9. New York and Washington state are explicit in prohibiting resale of policies to unlicensed entities. Washington's regulation is particularly strict. If a policy is transferred to any "person, custodian, investor, investor group, or other entity not holding such a license," that transfer is void as of the date of transfer, and all rights in the insurance policy are restored to the viator. Plus, the viator does not have to return the viatical settlement. See, RCW 48.102.045, [1995, c 161 § 9].

10. California doesn't explicitly prohibit resale to non-licensed entities. However the insurance department considers such sales to be illegal and claims the right to suspend or cancel the license of a company that does so. It also may void the sales contract. They claim the power to take these actions is granted in several sections of the Insurance Code. Since this is an interpretation and not explicit law, viatical companies are braced to challenge it in court, if necessary. What this means to investors is that such a sale is questionable.

11. That case was limited to charges by the SEC that an unlicensed viatical company, Life Partners, and its president, Brian Pardo, committed numerous violations of securities law, including fraud and misrepresentation. For details, see chapter 6 in *Cash for the Final Days* by Gloria G. Wolk.

CHAPTER THREE

❖

SIGNING UP

Viatical settlements were not known in the U.S. until the mid 1980's. Today this is a $600 million industry with two national trade organizations, 40 recognized viatical providers—and dozens of maverick companies. That's why it's important to know who you're dealing with, before you sign up.

L ETTERS FROM UNHAPPY INVESTORS GIVE SOME IDEA OF THE problems people have encountered in this unregulated industry. Here's a sampling. The first is from a Midwestern businessman, the second from a senior citizen in Florida.

Letter # 1

I bought a portion of a policy with an 18-month life expectancy. That was 28 months ago. I called the company to ask some questions. I was told I could sell my portion and that the agent I bought my portion from could help me. When I called him, he told me it couldn't be done and he was upset that somebody told me that. Who's lying? I just want my money back.

Letter # 2.

Somehow an agent found that I have money in an annuity that is coming due in a few more weeks. The agent gave me information about the viatical investment. As I get more involved I realize there is more to be known. Still, the concept is appealing from its humanitarian features and profitability.

* * *

Most people know little about viatical investments because most viatical companies don't want investors to know more. For example, investors are told that viaticals are as safe as CDs or annuities. If you ask in what way viaticals are like CDs, you'll be told with great conviction, "No Risk," or, "Guaranteed Principal."

Instead of rushing to write out a check, consider how you might react if a neighbor asked you to buy the death benefits of his/her life insurance. What would you need to know, what would you need to do, to make certain it was a safe investment? If you give some thought to this, you'll realize why investment advisors as well as individual investors need to have a clear understanding of the viatical process. Additionally, once your check is cashed, you have no control over the process. Therefore, ask questions and *get answers in writing*.

The following are questions from actual people who contacted the author when they did not get answers from sales agents or doubted the answers they were given.

QUESTIONS MOST OFTEN ASKED
(PLUS A FEW THAT SHOULD BE)

♦ How do viatical companies find viators?

♦ How are viators (sellers) screened?

♦ What is underwriting?

- How is purchase price determined?
- How is transfer of ownership recorded?
- What is a premium waiver?
- Who pays premiums?
- What safeguards assure that premiums are paid?
- What happens if the viator dies before premiums are depleted?
- What happens if the viator outlives his/her life expectancy?
- Are there other expenses?
- How safe is the escrow account?
- What are "policy services"?
- What is "viator tracking"?
- What proof is there that the viatical company actually has an insurance policy to sell?
- What proof is there that a viator actually is fatally ill?
- How does one learn about the viator's demise?
- Who submits the death claim?
- Can viators change their minds?
- Can investors change their minds?
- Do viators receive a fair deal from these investments?

HOW DO VIATICAL COMPANIES FIND VIATORS?

Viatical companies don't find viators. Many viators start the process with a phone call after reading an advertisement or hearing about viatical settlements from a referral source.

This is not to say that viatical companies sit patiently waiting for clients to phone. Thousands of dollars are spent for advertisements in disease-specific magazines and publications that target specific community groups, such as seniors and gays.

Viatical companies also produce audio and video tapes, conduct community seminars for disease-specific groups, maintain web sites on the Internet, and—most important—solicit referrals from *centers of influence*.

Centers of influence include

- Human resource managers
- Benefits counselors
- Ministers
- Employers
- Philanthropic organizations that service the terminally ill
- Insurance agents
- Financial planners
- Funeral directors
- Hospice operators
- Attorneys
- Doctors
- Bankers

To attract these referrals, viatical companies hold seminars at hospitals and business sites, send out promotional materials, and offer referral fees. Yes, doctors and lawyers get referral fees. And some don't wait for an offer. They demand it.[1]

HOW ARE VIATORS SCREENED?

Screening begins at the offices of the viatical company. The preselection process weeds out applicants that don't fit the company's guidelines; for example:

- *Illness.* Not all companies accept all illnesses.
- *Policy type.* Some policy types are unacceptable to the company.
- *Policy features.* Some features are likewise unacceptable.
- *Life expectancy.* Each company sets its own standard.

WHAT IS UNDERWRITING?

There are two major areas of risk: medical and insurance. Each area requires separate underwriting. Underwriting is how a company puts a price tag on risk. Underwriting begins with gathering medical and insurance information. After the home office staff does the preliminary analysis, information about selected viators is sent to the medical and insurance specialists who underwrite the risks. As a result of their analysis, the experts advise about a purchase price (or price range) commensurate with the risk.

Every viatical company claims strict *medical* underwriting. Insurance underwriting usually is limited to verification of coverage and disclosure of existing policy loans.

Verification of coverage (VOC) means that the insurer confirms that the policy is in force (it hasn't lapsed), it's past the contestable period, and it's assignable at full face value.[a]

This is inadequate protection for investors.[b]

HOW IS PURCHASE PRICE DETERMINED?

Purchase price is based *primarily* on medical and insurance underwriting. The other chief factor *should* be the mandated minimums set by some states or, as an alternative, minimums specified in the model viatical law drafted by The National Association of Insurance Commissioners (N.A.I.C.).[c] In essence, this law states that if life expectancy is X, the purchase price should be no lower than a certain percentage of the death benefit.[d]

This minimum should never be less than 50 percent of the death benefit. If a policy is offered with a price below 50 percent of the death benefit, something is wrong. Someone is being victimized. The victim may be the viator who is cheated of thousands of dollars. Or it may be the investor who has bought a policy that may never pay death benefits. To learn about policies that sell for 10 or 15 percent of the death benefit, see chapter 8, "Fraud

---

[a] Terms are explained in the glossary and in chapter 4.

[b] See chapters 5, 8, and 9.

[c] Complete details about purchase offers are in "Cash for the Final Days."

[d] Not all states have adopted the minimums set by the model designed by N.A.I.C.

Watch."

There are a number of other behind-the-scenes factors that influence purchase price (see chapter 4) but the last word belongs to the viator. Informed viators, which generally include those who sell through brokers, don't immediately accept or reject a purchase offer. They wait until all offers are made. Then there are negotiations as viatical companies try to outbid each other. Since there are more investors than policies for sale, bidding can be highly competitive. The law of supply and demand means that purchase price usually rises before an offer is accepted.

HOW IS TRANSFER OF OWNERSHIP RECORDED?

Once a viator accepts an offer, transfer papers are whisked to him/her by overnight delivery. These papers include

♦ The insurer's Absolute Assignment form [a]

♦ The insurer's Beneficiary Change form

♦ The viatical company's Release of Liability form

The release form must be signed by all current beneficiaries.[b] Most viatical companies require that signatures be notarized. Notarization ensures that an imposter didn't sign in place of an insured or a beneficiary.[2]

The release of liability is very important. Once beneficiaries sign and have it notarized, they no longer have legal standing to sue the company or the investor to recover their inheritance.[c]

Signed transfer papers are returned to the viatical company, copied, and sent by overnight delivery to the insurer. Then everyone waits for the insurer to return the forms showing the new policy owner(s) and beneficiary(ies).

Investors should receive copies of all documents. If you're the sole owner, you should receive the original insurance policy or certificate of insurance (for

---

[a] This form assigns all rights of the policy to a new owner.

[b] Release of Liability may be called "Release of Beneficial Interest."

[c] The exception would be if the entire transaction is illegal. See chapter 8, "Fraud Watch."

a group policy). If you're a co-owner, you should receive a copy of these documents.[a]

WHAT IS A PREMIUM WAIVER?

Another name for premium waiver is *disability waiver of premium*. This is a rider—an add-on to the policy. The rider stipulates that premiums are waived (excused) after the insured has been totally disabled for six months.

Disability premium waivers have become as common to employer group policies as they are to personally owned insurance. In either case, the insurance company requires on-going proof of continuing disability. Thus, the waiver must be renewed annually. Renewal usually requires signatures from the viator *and* the treating physician.

If a policy does not include a premium waiver, premiums must be paid. At times the policy includes this rider, but the viator didn't apply to have the waiver activated. Or the viator may have been unaware of the rider, or is not yet eligible since he/she has not been totally disabled for six months.

In these situations, the viatical company or its escrow agent applies to activate the waiver, when it's appropriate to do so. This can only be done with the cooperation of the insured and the insured's physician.[b]

Investors may be told that the premium waiver will save them from the obligation to pay premiums, if the viator outlives life expectancy. Don't count on this. Premiums will have to be paid if the insured disappears, or if the policy is resold and the insured refuses to cooperate with new investors, or the physician is uncooperative.

WHO PAYS PREMIUMS?

The viator pays premiums. The cost of future premiums is subtracted from

---

[a] For viator's confidentiality, names of original beneficiaries, the viator's current address and place of employment should be blocked out.

[b] If the viator returns to work, even part-time, the premium waiver no longer applies.

the purchase price before an offer is made to the viator.[a] These funds are placed in an escrow or custody account.

HOW MUCH IS SET ASIDE FOR PREMIUMS?

Each company has its own formula for determining the amount set aside for premiums (see chapter 4 for details).

Other factors are unique to each viator and his/her policy. The premium for one viator may be ten times the amount for another viator who has the same type of policy, issued by the same insurer. Cost depends on

- Type of insurance (i.e., term or cash value; group or private)
- Amount of death benefit
- Age of the insured at the time the policy was issued (or current age, if the policy is renewable term insurance)
- Whether the insured was rated[b]
- Riders that add benefits (e.g., accidental death benefit)
- Whether the policy is renewable or re-entry term insurance[3]

WHAT SAFEGUARDS ASSURE THAT PREMIUMS ARE PAID?

You won't know whether premiums are paid unless you build safeguards to keep you informed. Here are a few ways to do this:

- Ask the viatical company to send a notice each time a premium is paid.
- Ask the viatical company for copies of canceled checks.
- Insist that these conditions be added to the agreement/contract with the viatical company.
- Ask the insurer to send duplicate premium notices and copies of annual statements to you.

One investor who phoned the insurer to find out if premiums were up-

---

[a] Viators must be quoted a net offer—the full amount they will receive.

[b] Rated means charged more for being a sub-standard risk.

to-date was told that the premium had increased but the escrow agent had paid the same as the previous year—not enough to keep the policy in force. The investor contacted his co-investors to arrange direct payment of premiums based on each investor's pro rata share.

Warning: If premiums are not paid on time, the policy will lapse. If investors don't know that a premium wasn't paid, they will lose their entire investment.

WHAT HAPPENS IF THE VIATOR DIES BEFORE PREMIUMS ARE DEPLETED?

If the viator dies sooner than expected, there may be unused premiums in the escrow account, but don't expect a refund. Viatical companies claim the right to apply this excess to other policies that exceed life expectancy.

However, these unspent funds are used at the option of the viatical companies. They also have the option to pocket the cash—with the exception of one of the examined companies, which commits in writing to apply excess premiums to other policies.[a]

WHAT HAPPENS IF THE VIATOR OUTLIVES HIS/HER LIFE EXPECTANCY?

If the viator lives longer than expected, premiums in the reserve account will be depleted. Then *investors* must pay to keep the policy in force. If premiums are not paid, the policy could lapse.

Far more serious is the situation of co-ownership with say, 10 strangers, when some of these strangers don't pay their share of premiums. This happened to a number of investors who purchased fractionalized shares of policies through Life Partners, Inc. (LPI).[b]

When these co-owners didn't pay, LPI sent letters to investors warning them that their shares would be sold for the cost of premiums. In other words, these clients would lose their principal and someone else would have

---

[a] See chapter 4, "Contracts Compared."

[b] Life Partners coined this term to refer to co-ownership.

an instant profit.[a]

ARE THERE OTHER EXPENSES?

Investors rarely learn about other expenses until long after their checks are cashed.

Policy loans are one example. If the insured had a cash value policy with an outstanding policy loan, and if the loan is not paid off at the time of closing (transfer), the insurer will bill for annual loan interest. The question is Who bears this expense, investors or viators?

There is no standard procedure. It's likely the viatical company will deduct from the viaticum an amount equal to loan interest, using the same formula as for premiums. These monies *probably* will go into the escrow or "premium reserve account." Should the viator outlive his/her life expectancy, investors *probably* will be burdened with loan interest.[4]

Loan interest is not the only expense. Although nearly every contract implies or actually states "no expenses" beyond the initial purchase price, there may be fees for tracking (monitoring the viator) and for servicing the policy. See chapter 4, "Contracts Compared."

HOW SAFE IS THE ESCROW ACCOUNT?

Every viatical company—including illegal ones—uses an escrow trust account, supposedly to keep investors' funds safe until the transaction is completed. The problem is not all escrow accounts are equal.

When the mavericks of the industry claim to use an escrow trust, these accounts usually are private trusts managed by the viatical company's partner or similar cohort. A true-life example of this is described in chapter 9.

In other cases the escrow trust is set up in a lawyer's name. This is very dangerous to investors. Should the law firm become insolvent, a bankruptcy court might consider all funds in this account to be assets of the attorney.

---

[a] From information obtained by the SEC in their legal pursuit of Life Partners.

To learn how legitimate viatical companies safeguard investor funds, see chapter 4, "Contracts Compared."

WHAT ARE "POLICY SERVICES"?

Policy services may be as simple as paying premiums or making address changes: the investor-owner's, or the viator's. Or they may include filing for disability waiver of premium, or converting a group policy to an individual one. Policy services do include filing the death certificate and death claim with the insurer and may include distributing the proceeds to co-owners. See chapter 4 for details.

WHAT IS "VIATOR TRACKING"?

If nothing happened between the closing of escrow on the sale of the policy and the viator's demise, it would be sufficient to ask the viator's physician to notify the viatical company when a death certificate is available. But viators need to be tracked from the time they transfer their policies. One reason is that premium waivers must be renewed annually. Renewal requires a physician's signature and usually the viator's signature as well. This is true of all policies, whether individually owned or group.

Some companies use the U.S. mail to do tracking. Viators are given postcards and instructions to return one card each month. The postcards ask for an updated address, telephone number, and doctors' information. Yes, it seems as if the viator is dropping a line to say, "Hi, I'm not dead yet."

Other companies ask for "designated contact persons" (relatives and/or friends), and permission to contact them on a rotating basis. Depending on life expectancy, these people may be contacted monthly or quarterly.

Some companies contract with American Viatical Services (AVS) to perform tracking. And others turn to AVS belatedly—to hunt a viator who has disappeared. Philip Loy, president of AVS, made this observation:

At least 30 percent of people who get a viatical settlement a major life change and move: to live nearer their family, or from New York

to Arizona for the climate, then back again—it was too damn hot.
And they may not have the same physician when they move back.
They have to be monitored every month, or you lose track. It doesn't
take long for a person to escape, and you may lose the ability to
follow them. And, you don't get paid without a death certificate.

How do you find a viator who has disappeared? Sometimes through a
search of hospices and funeral parlors; sometimes through a skip-trace service
with access to the databases of the U.S. Postal Service and the Social Security
Administration.

Sometimes there are clues that a viator is likely to disappear. According
to Philip Loy of AVS,

> You can see hints this will happen in the medical record, before a
> policy is viaticated. Such as the time I asked the attending physician,
> "Is this the kind of person who would go into the desert and just die
> and not leave a note?"
>
> The doctor's reply: "This isn't the kind of person to do that. This IS
> the person."

Some viatical companies allow investors to do their own tracking.[a]
However, if tracking is done for you, be sure that details are spelled out in the
purchase contract: when, where, how; how often, and lastly, by whom you will
be notified of the death of the viator.

WHAT PROOF IS THERE THAT THE COMPANY ACTUALLY HAS A POLICY TO SELL?

There is no proof that you are buying an actual policy. You either trust the
viatical company or do some sleuthing: verify coverage for yourself.[b]

The problem is you can't check anything—whether a policy is real or that

---

[a] See chapter 4, "Contracts Compared."

[b] For details, see chapter 7.

it's legally transferable or that it hasn't lapsed or that the insured didn't commit fraud on the application—until after closing (policy transfer). It's a situation ripe for abuse and it underscores the importance of investing with established, licensed companies.[a]

When you have the original policy in your possession, you can phone the insurer's home office to confirm the face amount and premium information.[b] Don't be disappointed if the company refuses to give information over the telephone. For confidentiality reasons, many insurers send this information by mail.

If you're a co-owner, you should receive a photocopy of the policy. Once the transfer takes place and you are listed as irrevocable beneficiary, you can ask the insurer to verify insurance information.

What if you find there is no viator? One way to avoid Ponzi/pyramid schemes is to stay clear of viatical "marketing" companies. See chapter 9, "Fraud Watch," for tips on recognizing a con artist.

WHAT PROOF IS THERE THAT A VIATOR ACTUALLY IS FATALLY ILL?

Investors have no proof that a viator is really dying. Medical records can be faked not only by so-called viatical companies but by viators (see chapter 6, "Predicting Life Expectancy"). Then again, it's likely you won't be given actual and complete medical records. If you did receive the full medical record, often two inches thick, it's the rare investor who would find these records meaningful.

The following sample is taken from marketing materials sent to prospective investors.[c] The bold type is exactly as printed in the original, which had the insured's name blocked out (although two other summaries in the kit had full names of the insureds—as if someone was careless and allowed

---

[a] See chapter 8 for details about a viatical Ponzi scheme: no policies existed.

[b] You can get the toll free number for the insurer by calling 1-800-555-1212.

[c] From a Utah-based company that doesn't buy policies but markets to investors.

investors to have more information that they were entitled to).[a]

Sample Medical Report

Insured's Name: **XXXXXX** [sic]
Insured's Age: 31   Life Expectancy: 24 months
Insurance Company: Northwestern Mutual
Face amount: $75,000   Total Purchase Price: $58,593.75

Total Return: **28%** [sic]

Current medicals-Insured has experienced the following:
T-Cell is 260	Persistent cough
HIV Wasting Syndrome	Severe Depression
Non Responsive to AZT	Fatigue
Lymphoid Pneumonia	Memory Loss
Continued Drug Abuse	

Patient has tried Protease Inhibitor but was a non-responder. The AIDS virus is still present in lymph tissue, & is growing stronger.

****

On the basis of this report, would you invest? Although the report is typically sparse, it reveals enough to cause some concern. Note the symptom "memory loss." This might indicate doubt about the viator's legal competency. If the viator was not legally competent to enter into a contract, named beneficiaries could challenge the legality of the sale after the viator's demise (see chapter 5).

Firms that show medical records to investors may show you something similar to the above sample. Other companies provide nothing more than a diagnosis and life expectancy report. Still others provide summaries of drug therapies, hospitalizations, and so forth. These summaries may satisfy a lay person but usually are inadequate to submit to a specialist for a second opinion.

---

[a] Since this is not the only company that displayed *some* viators' names, Social Security numbers, and policy numbers, one has to wonder about this carelessness.

HOW DOES ONE LEARN ABOUT THE VIATOR'S DEMISE?

The company responsible for tracking the viator is charged with the duty to inform investors of the viator's death.

WHO SUBMITS THE DEATH CLAIM?

The viatical firm or its agent handles details such as submitting death claims. This responsibility should be spelled out in the viatical contract.

CAN VIATORS CHANGE THEIR MINDS?

Viators can change their minds about the sale if they live in a state with viatical regulation, or they arrange the sale with a licensed viatical company. Viatical laws permit viators a grace period in which they can rescind (cancel) the sale. Most grace periods allow cancellation within 30 days of signing transfer of ownership or 15 days of receiving the viaticum. If a viator changes his/her mind after closing, all funds must be returned.

CAN INVESTORS CHANGE THEIR MINDS?

Most legitimate companies permit investors to withdraw their money if funds have not yet been paid to a viator. But there are conditions—and costs (see chapter 4).

DO VIATORS RECEIVE A FAIR DEAL FROM THESE INVESTMENTS?

Sometimes viators receive a fair settlement amount, but not always. For details, see appendix VI.

The other major concern of viators is confidentiality. Viators worry that their policies will be resold to a group of individual investors who might phone them—or their relatives—to find out if they are still alive. They imagine as many as 20 investors phoning. This is not paranoia. It has happened.

END NOTES

1. Pamela Sherrid, "Enriching the Final Days," *U.S. News & World Report,* August 25, 1996. Probably as a result of this revelation many states that recently enacted viatical regulation included a prohibition against payment of referral fees to professionals whose primary role is advisor or caretaker to the viator.

2. Notaries can be found at many business supply stores, banks, and privately owned mail box businesses. Notaries are individuals who are state certified to authenticate the identity of the individual signing a form. Identity checks may be satisfied with a birth certificate, passport, and/or driver's license.

3. Renewable or re-entry term means that the insured must qualify medically for the lower rate. If the insured has a serious medical problem, premiums could increase 30 times higher than those paid during the last term period.

4. Loan interest usually is payable annually. The interest may be fixed or a variable rate, depending on the policy. The interest rate should be stated in the policy.

CHAPTER FOUR

❖

CONTRACTS COMPARED

> "The Lender understands and agrees that all interest or earnings, if any, on funds held by custodian prior to the purchase of Benefits shall inure to the Trustee for administrative fees and costs . . . ."

T HE ABOVE QUOTE IS FROM AN ACTUAL VIATICAL CONTRACT. IT demonstrates the first lesson: Contracts are drafted for the protection of the contract writer. Yet in most contracts there are standard terms, clauses, and conditions. These occur because most transactions are regulated to some extent by state or federal law.

Consider the contracts for mutual funds and other regulated investments, or real estate, automobile sales, or insurance of any kind. These are regulated and must include certain standard provisions.

None of this is true of viaticals. Since there are no state or federal rules that apply to viatical investments, each viatical company makes its own rules. The result: Each viatical investment contract is unique. Thus, the investor is the "buyer" in one contract, "lender" in another, and something else in yet another contract.

Once you get a grasp of these terms, you are ready for the hard part: understanding the contract. Although some viatical contracts are as brief and simple as a receipt for money, others are written in such a way that no sane person could understand them. The following story shows some of the problems investors can expect.

Mal, an insurance agent and stockbroker for more than two decades, trotted up to the door of my friend's home one bright sunny Saturday morning. He was dressed as if for a funeral and toted a briefcase stuffed with papers from two different viatical companies. One was the legitimate company whose brochure he had sent in the mail.[a] The other was a marketing company that offered investors a choice between its standard agreement and a "Trust." The trust guaranteed a return of 30 percent for "36-month paper" (as Mal termed it).

This guarantee was made possible by means of a surety bond that paid principal plus 30 percent interest, if the viator lived past 36 months. The downside was the possible loss of greater profit, if the viator died earlier than 36 months. Investors were stuck with the guarantee—no more, no less.

The insurer, Mal said in answer to our questions, was a property-liability carrier based in the Cayman Islands and licensed in Michigan. I asked if the insurer were licensed in California, since this is where we were doing business. Mal changed the subject. After several attempts to get back to the question, Mal finally said, "I'm sure they're licensed here."

That was all. Mal firmly resisted providing us with details about the

---

[a] The legitimate company is one whose contract is analyzed here.

insurance company that backed the surety bond. Instead, he bragged that the viatical company offering the surety bond was firm about not accepting life policies with ratings lower than "A-."

But when I looked at the back of the one-page contract, I found this:

> **All life insurance policies shall be issued by B+ or better rated insurance companies, as determined by A.M. Best.**

Mal was flabbergasted. "That can't be." He pondered this aloud, reminding us that the trailer on the video he showed us had clearly stated that ratings were "A-" or better. Clearly flustered, Mal refused to look at the back of the contract where that sentence was printed. His discomfort implied that none of Mal's other prospective investors had questioned him about the statement.

When asked what other investors were buying, Mal said that "no one went for the bond." Everyone wanted to take a chance at higher yields.

The front side of the contract offered a choice of two investment plans. "Traditional Plans" were described in terms of life expectancies and projected yields, choices similar to those of other viatical companies but with one exception. I asked Mal what this meant:

> $_____ Contestable (market rate-call for quote) $_____
> (The dollar amounts were to be filled in by the sales agent.)

Mal didn't know what was meant by "contestable." I pointed to a similar statement on the back of the application:

> **All life insurance policies shall be non-contestable. *This does not apply to contestable plans.* [sic]**

Mal seemed honestly mystified. He should have read his marketing materials before setting out to make a sale. Later, when I read through the marketing packet, I found this explanation:

> . . . the contestable program involves life insurance policies
> purchased within the contestable period. These transactions
> can produce returns as high as 100%. They bear the risk,
> however, of the life insurance company contesting the claim
> should the Viator's demise occur within the contestable period
> . . . Effective due diligence combined with an expeditious
> policy replacement program can mitigate this risk.

What is meant by "effective due diligence"? It didn't appear that any due diligence was exercised if the statement referred to policies that were within the two-year contestability period. Anyone who buys a policy that is within the contestability period bears the risk that the insurer will void the policy for cause. This is certain to happen if the insured dies during the contestability period.

Even if these insureds died long after the contestability period, the insurer may have cause to void the policy for "material misrepresentation"—fraud. Fraud seemed likely since:

♦ These viator applied for insurance less than two years ago

♦ Now these insureds were terminally ill

Each of these viators would have to be one of those *rare* cases of someone diagnosed with a serious, life-threatening illness shortly after a new life insurance policy is issued. How is it possible that one viatical company has a quantity of such policies, unless fraud is a component?

Under these circumstances, it's intriguing to speculate what the company means by "expeditious policy replacement program."

These stories should convince you of the importance of looking carefully at every word of the contract. Don't get trapped into buying a policy that was issued on the basis of a fraudulent insurance application.

As described above, this contract wasn't easily understood. Although it offered little information to investors, the application process was simple: one page of large print and boxes to check and lines to fill in with dollar amounts. On the back of this tissue-thin pink paper was all the information the company willingly gave investors—in tiny type.

By contrast, the legitimate companies used for our comparison have, without exception, multi-page applications. Not that this is preferable. If there is too much to read or the task seems laborious, investors don't read. This is common with mutual fund prospectuses. People don't read them. But mutual funds are highly regulated securities. These regulations protect investors from swindlers and undisclosed risks.

Contracts from the following companies, which are deemed to be legitimate, are used in this comparative analysis: [a]

— Dedicated Resources

— LifeLine

— AMG

— ALI

— Legacy Capital

— Viatical Benefactors

No doubt there will be other contracts that you peruse. Over time there will be other legitimate companies, and the companies listed above may alter their contracts, as well. Despite changes, you can use these techniques as a guide to evaluating any viatical investment opportunity.

CRITERIA

These selected companies meet the following criteria:

♦ *Length of time in the viatical business:* Either the viatical company or its parent has been in business for several years.[b]

♦ *Direct buyers:* The viatical company or its parent buys directly from viators.

♦ *Direct sellers:* Investors and investment advisors can go directly to the

---

[a] The comparison offered here does not include illegal companies—the "mavericks" described by Per Larson in appendix VI.

[b] See appendix II.

company, rather than do business through a marketing company[a]

♦ *Licensing.* The viatical company or its parent is approved to do business in states that require a viatical license in order to transact business with viators[b]

♦ *Securities compliance.* The company is registered with the state department in charge of securities in those states that require such registration[c]

The above is not a pick-and-choose menu. Viatical companies should meet all criteria. At the same time these criteria are not all-inclusive. For example, licensing is only a starting point.

One reason that a viatical license should be viewed as nothing more than a starting point is that licensed viatical companies don't always act ethically or legally. One prominent licensed viatical company (now defunct) committed several violations of viatical law. Another, which was known to regulators as an unsavory company, slipped through the net and now boasts of having a viatical license in California.[1] A third, now licensed in Florida, claimed it fired two principals whose checkered pasts would not have passed Florida's requisite background investigation.[d] However, a phone call to that company will reach these same "fired" principals.[2] Although these companies offer investments to the public, for obvious reasons they are not included in the following evaluation.

A FURTHER WORD ABOUT LICENSING

Why should a company based in Florida or New Mexico have a license from

---

[a] These companies may also sell through marketing companies.

[b] States with viatical regulation generally allow applicants to transact business if their applications are not rejected in 60 days.

[c] No attempt was made to verify if these companies are registered to sell securities in the states where policies are resold to investors.

[d] See chapter 8, "Fraud Watch."

California, New York, or Washington, if the company only does business in its home state?

The reason is that viatical settlements are not a local nor are they strictly a regional business. This is a nation-wide industry and it's spreading internationally.

THE COMPANIES/THEIR INVESTOR ARMS

Most licensed viatical companies don't market investments under their original names. Funding firm, Dedicated Resources, is unique in that it sells to investors under its own name. Other licensed viatical companies sprouted branches—investor arms. These firms and their investor arms are Legacy Benefits d/b/a Legacy Capital, Neuma d/b/a as AMG, Page and Associates d/b/a LifeLine, Affirmative Lifestyles d/b/a Affirmative Lifestyles, Inc. Viatical Funding (ALI), and Independent Benefits d/b/a Viatical Benefactors.[a]

Reasons for separate investor arms include

- *Expense*: If a company is audited, the audit process is less cumbersome and less expensive for separate entities than for a merged one
- *Future regulation:* Tax and legal requirements change frequently. If the investor arm is found to be noncompliant, this won't injure the reputation of the parent company.
- *Current regulation*: Licensed viatical brokers are not allowed to buy policies directly from viators.

This is why two licensed brokers on this list grew these funding arms: Affirmative Lifestyles d/ba/ALI, and Independent Benefits d/ba/ Viatical Benefactors.

LARGE PRINT/SMALL PRINT

You may have heard the adage, *Large print is what they want you to know; small print is what they don't want you to know.* Viatical contracts have pages and pages

---

[a] The acronym *d/b/a* means, "doing business as."

of small print. To make matters worse, nothing is standard—not the language, not the terms or conditions. One viatical company refers to itself as "Maker,"another as "Seller," another as "Agent," and so on. This lack of uniformity is evident in references made to the contracts: one company uses "Section A, B, C" while another uses roman numerals to separate the sections of the contract, and so on.

Although some sections *appear* to be "standard" fare, don't skip them. One word could completely change the meaning.

Language and terms may be misleading and sometimes contradictory. Read everything—carefully. For maximum benefit, keep the contract you're considering close at hand as you read this chapter.

COMMON INFORMATION

Each of the contracts reviewed includes the following information:
- Minimum purchase price
- Policy requirements[a]
- Requirements that viators must be terminally ill and of sound mind[b]
- Independent medical evaluations
- Requirement that beneficiaries sign waivers of interest[c]
- State guarantee fund described as added protection
- Escrow information: names and qualifications of trustees and/or agents charged with duties of escrow, policy servicing, and/or tracking
- Bank information: name and reputation of the bank that holds the escrow account
- Application for retirement account

---

[a] See chapter 5 for details.

[b] See chapter 5 for details.

[c] The exception is AMG. If a beneficiary is not available to sign this waiver, AMG obtains "an affidavit from the viator acknowledging his or her intent to dispossess them of their interest in the policy."

One last item exists in some form or other in each agreement: a "hold harmless" clause. This clause is used to discourage lawsuits. When you sign this, you agree not to blame the viatical company or the escrow agent for anything other than willful wrongdoing or gross negligence.

Beyond these common topics, agreements vary widely. Some companies provide information not found in other contracts (e.g., risk disclosure). Some ask for information not asked for by others (e.g., investor's net worth/suitability for this investment or investor's contingent beneficiary).

Differences make it hard to compare contracts. However, information from one company can be used to get similar information from another. If an investor phones a viatical company for information, he/she should request all answers in writing. This way, the answers become part of the contract.[a]

POLICY OWNER

The first question to ask is: Who will be the policy owner once the purchase is completed? [b]

Ownership means the policy belongs to and is the asset of the owner. Ownership is control. A policy owner can withdraw the cash value of the policy, pledge the policy for a loan, incur liens against it, add beneficiaries, collect dividends, sell a policy, and do just about anything—except cancel an irrevocable beneficiary.[c]

When a viatical company or its agent is named owner, there is the additional risk that the policy will become subject to creditor's liens, including claims in divorce or bankruptcy court.

Life Partners (LPI) routinely took ownership until a federal court ordered

---

[a] Contracts and agreements can be changed in almost any situation. Since this industry is not regulated, no government agency has to approve changes.

[b] Another name for policy owner is policy holder.

[c] See appendix VII for an example of a viatical company that owned investors' policies and decided to sell the policies for less than the investment.

them to stop—for this very reason.[3] Other companies continue to take ownership, claiming that the court's ruling applied only to Life Partners. Yet once a viator receives the viaticum, there's no legal or practical reason for viatical companies to continue to own the policy.

When there are multiple/partial owners, some arrangement must be made for policy servicing. Who will do this? You? Or one of the other 20 with whom you co-own the policy?[4]

Most companies assign ownership to the viatical company or its agent.[a] The following illustrates how Assignment is done, when co-investors are "partial" beneficiaries:

At Viatical Benefactors, the viator ("Seller") transfers ownership to the licensed viatical company, who is owner/assignee throughout the sale process. The reason for this is to comply with the Health Insurance and Portability Act of 1996. The Act requires viators to sell to licensed viatical companies—not unlicensed investors—or risk being taxed on the viatical settlement.

Aaron Kokol of Viatical Benefactors explained that once the sale/transfer is complete, the policy can be reassigned (resold) without triggering tax consequences for the viator.[b]

However, this second transfer from Viatical Benefactors is not made to investors. Instead, reassignment of ownership is to the "Escrow Agent on behalf of Seller." [c]

A similar arrangement occurs at Legacy Capital where the escrow agent

becomes the nominal owner or assignee in trust for the investors and the investor becomes the beneficiary.[d]

---

[a] Policy servicing is explained in chapter 3.

[b] Via telephone interview.

[c] Page 6 section "Five" of Viatical Benefactors' contract.

[d] Page 1, Section 2, of the contract, and Page 2 of appendix A of Legacy's contract.

At Dedicated Resources, if

> the purchaser elects to be a partial Irrevocable Beneficiary of an asset
> . . . Dedicated Resources and/or its Assignees will become the owner
> of the policy. . . .[a]

ALI makes no mention of ownership. Since this is a limited partnership, it's likely that the partnership is owner. If you choose to invest with ALI, get this information *in writing*.

At LifeLine, the escrow agent is named as owner of the policy if the agent performs policy services.[b]

By contrast, AMG reassigns the policy to investors who then grant AMG "a limited power of attorney" for the purpose of policy servicing. For co-investors, this appears to be the safest approach of all current practices.[c]

If you have no choice but to allow another entity to assume ownership, be absolutely certain that you are listed as irrevocable beneficiary. Otherwise, you may have nothing to show for your money.

Which brings us to the next issue: *Who is beneficiary?*

WHO IS IRREVOCABLE BENEFICIARY?

Irrevocable means that it cannot be changed without the written consent of the (irrevocable) beneficiary.[d] Investors should be designated as irrevocable beneficiaries. But at AMG, the escrow trust is the irrevocable beneficiary. This is how AMG describes it:

> The trust will be sole and irrevocable beneficiary under the
> Policy which it holds for the beneficiaries of the Trust pursuant

---

[a] Page 2, Article One, number 6 of Dedicated's contract.

[b] Page 2, V, of LifeLine's contract.

[c] Page 1, Section 1, number 2 of AMG's contract.

[d] A life insurance policy can have both irrevocable and revocable beneficiaries.

to the Trust agreement, Exhibit "A" hereto.[a]

At Viatical Benefactors, although the escrow agent is irrevocable beneficiary during the sale/transfer process, the policy is reassigned to investors as irrevocable beneficiaries at the time of closing.

ALI, whose investment program is set up as a limited partnership, makes no mention of beneficiaries. It's likely that the partnership is beneficiary, but it may be the escrow company or another entity. If you invest with ALI, be sure to get the answer in writing.

MINIMUM PURCHASE PRICE

Viatical Benefactors has the lowest minimum purchase price: $5,000. AMG requires $10,000; Legacy Capital, Dedicated Resources, and LifeLine require $20,000. ALI'S limited partnership restricts participation to people and organizations with a net worth of at least $1 million who have at least $200,000 to invest.

POLICY RATINGS

Policies purchases are limited to those issued by solvent insurance companies. Solvency is judged by the ratings given insurance companies by independent rating services (Best's, Standard & Poor's, Moody's).

ALI doesn't state the minimum policy rating acceptable. Dedicated Resources and Legacy Capital require policies rated no lower than "A."

Viatical Benefactors restricts purchases to companies that are rated at least "A-." AMG accepts "A-" but will consider lower ratings if the face amount is covered by the state guarantee fund. Contradictory information is offered by LifeLine: Their contract states "A-," but their brochure and their Web site state "B."

---

[a] Page 1, number 3(d) of AMG's contract.

LIFE EXPECTANCY

Each company sets its own requirements for acceptable life expectancy of viators. Companies may buy policies from viators with longer life expectancies for their own portfolios, but this is what they offer investors.

Dedicated Resources and AMG accept life expectancies up to three years; ALI, Viatical Benefactors, and LifeLine accept up to four years; Legacy Capital, five years. See chapter 5 for other viator and policy requirements.

ESCROW INFORMATION

The escrow account and the manager of that account, also known as "escrow agent" or "trustee," are equally important.

Escrow agents or trustees (the terms are used interchangeably) are charged with the safekeeping and disbursement of purchase funds, viaticum, and policy premiums. They do not give advice, opinions, or make independent decisions. Nor are they required to advance funds if premium accounts run dry. They are simply record keepers and check-writers.

Of supreme importance for investors is to assure that escrow agents (whether individuals or companies) are third-party entities paid a fee for their services. They should not share the profits of the business.

Several viatical firms provide profiles of the escrow companies and agents they use, and one company supplies a copy of the bond for its escrow agent. Dedicated Resources is the only company that uses a bank trustee, who happens to be from the same bank that holds the escrow account.

Beware if the escrow account is set up in the name of an individual, a law firm, or an accounting firm.

Your investment may be small, but it will be flung into a pile of thousands of dollars paid by other investors. Those thousands could become millions. This is incredible temptation for anyone in control of these funds.

And, there are other considerations: The private firm might go out of business. Your funds, tucked safely in its asset account, would be frozen during the bankruptcy. Then there is the problem of commingling of investor funds. Commingling—mixing investor funds—appears to be routine with all viatical companies. For investors, the concern is that F.D.I.C. insurance applies only to amounts up to $100,000.[a] This figure is *per account*. There is no insurance for amounts that exceed $100,000 in any one account. If your investment is commingled with other funds and the total is greater than $100,000, F.D.I.C. insurance will not protect the excess.

One alternative is to have separate escrow accounts at the same bank. This way, F.D.I.C. insurance applies to each account. But will the viatical company go to the trouble and expense of doing this? Investors (and investment advisors) should ask.

As for the escrow account itself, legitimate viatical companies use a nationally or federally chartered bank.[b]

ALI's account is at Bank One, Texas, N.A., in Austin, Texas.[c] Dedicated Resources has a custody account with Comerica Bank and Trust, F.S.B., which is described as "the 25th largest bank holding company in the nation."[d]

LifeLine uses Northern Trust Corporation, a Chicago-based, multibank holding company with subsidiaries in many states.

Legacy Capital and Viatical Benefactors use Star Bank N.A., of Cleveland, Ohio, one of the largest banks in Ohio.

AMG uses Citibank, FSB, described as one of the two largest financial institutions in the world. According to David-Irwin Binter, president of AMG and Neuma, "I would be comfortable to have hundreds of millions of dollars at Citibank."

---

[a] F.D.I.C. means Federal Deposit Insurance Corporation.

[b] Don't be lured into trusting a viatical company simply because it uses a federally chartered bank for the escrow account. According to San Francisco-based attorney Gerry H. Goldsholle, "Anyone can use a bank to handle ministerial functions. This could be `window dressing' for what is essentially a corrupt operation."

[c] "N.A." after a bank name means North America.

[d] "F.S.B." after a bank name means Federal Savings Bank.

INTEREST-BEARING ESCROW

Is the escrow trust an interest-bearing account? If yes, do investors get to keep this interest? As my friend remarked to salesman Mal, "If the company keeps the interest, there is no incentive for them to place your money quickly." Mal had no response.

Unlike Mal, four of the five examined companies address this issue. ALI uses a noninterest-bearing account.[a] Viatical Benefactors uses an account that currently pays 3 percent on nonqualified monies.[b] Both of these companies separate interest earned on purchase price from interest earned on premiums. Interest earned on premiums is used "to satisfy any overdue maturities,"[c] while interest on purchase funds is returned to the investor.[d]

Dedicated Resources,[e] LifeLine, and Legacy Capital keep all interest that accrues on funds held prior to purchase and are silent about interest earned on premiums.[f] AMG does not address the issue.

EXPENSES

Most contracts include words to the effect that there are no further expenses beyond the initial purchase price. LifeLine's contract, for example, states,

> The cost and fees for all services . . . shall be complete and inclusive in the policy purchase price.

---

[a] Page 9 of ALI's contract.

[b] Nonqualified means not tax deductible, not part of an IRA, Keogh, or other tax deductible retirement plan.

[c] Page 6 of the contract

[d] As stated on a separate, noncontractual page supplied by Viatical Benefactors: "Five Questions to ask any Viatical Company." [sic]

[e] Page 2, number 2(d) of the contract.

[f] LifeLine's contract: page 2, section VII, D; Legacy Capital's contract: page 4, section 9 (b).

Later, in the same contract LifeLine states,

Administrative fees may be deducted from . . . funds prior to policy closing.

Since administrative fees are deducted from these funds before viators are paid, the effect is that viators are paying these expenses. Viatical Benefactors describes it this way:

> Monies used to buy the actual death benefit and related benefits of a life insurance policy, are net of operating and administrative costs.

A quick reading of this and other contracts gives the impression that purchase price is all-inclusive. Not necessarily. Several paragraphs later Viatical Benefactors absolves themselves of responsibility for any fees charged by the escrow agency. This is true of other companies, as well. It not only implies but permits billing by the escrow agency. And there are likely to be fees for policy services and tracking, as well as postlife expectancy expenses.

POLICY SERVICES AND TRACKING

Two companies—LifeLine and Dedicated Resources—allow investors to do their own policy servicing and tracking. Before choosing this option consider everything that might go wrong, especially if a viator disappears.

Neither of these two contracts mentions the possibility of investors who start out doing policy servicing and tracking, and have a mind change. Will these companies accept the responsibility three months or a year later? If so, at what cost? *Get the answer in writing.*

If you prefer to have LifeLine manage policy services and tracking from the onset of your agreement, there is a fee. Policy services cost $100 a year, and tracking is $325 per policy, per year. Co-owners share the tracking fee. While pay-as-you-go may appear more costly than companies that claim not to charge for these services, it may be safer for investors. Tracking can be expensive. Pay-as-you-go assures there are funds to pay for these services. By contrast, if expenses are part of administrative cost deducted at closing, the company may redirect these funds to other expenses when its cash flow is weak.

Although Dedicated Resources gives investors the option to handle tracking, if you prefer to turn this over to the viatical company there is no cost for *ordinary* tracking.

AMG does not charge for *ordinary* policy service or tracking.

Legacy Capital covers *ordinary* policy servicing and tracking at no extra cost, up to "the midpoint of life expectancy, times 1.5."

When asked about this concept—midpoint of life expectancy— Meir Eliav, president of Legacy explained it this way:

> If life expectancy is 24 months, the midpoint is 12 months. Multiple 12 months by 1.5, and the result is 18 months. This is the time during which Legacy covers policy servicing and tracking for a viator whose life expectancy is 24 months.

Investors are charged when services are beyond ordinary, such as converting a group policy to an individual policy. Then Legacy Capital expects

> the Investor will also be responsible for payment, to the Escrow Agent, of the fees related to the collection, payment and administration of the premium.[a]

ALI charges annual, ongoing fees "not expected to exceed 4 percent" of total death benefits. This pre-established charges cover all services.[b]

POSTLIFE EXPECTANCY EXPENSES

If a viator lives well beyond life expectancy, investors must be prepared to keep cash flowing to support their investment. For example, Legacy Capital

---

[a] Page 4, section 10 of the contract.

[b] Page 13 of the contract.

provides policy services and tracking for the period of life expectancy at no charge, but reserves the right to turn these services over to another entity if the viator outlives life expectancy. Then,

> the investor shall be responsible for paying any fees required by such entity, to perform the tracking duty [a]

By contrast, Dedicated Resources promises to continue policy services

> at no additional cost, unless otherwise stated herein . . .

Since no additional costs are stated, presumably there are no other costs. But watch for contract changes.

AMG, referring to an itemized list of policy services and tracking, appears to provide these services indefinitely.

If LifeLine investors elect to have the company manage policy servicing and tracking (remember: there's an extra charge), it's likely these services will continue postlife expectancy. What isn't clear is whether the company will continue these services at the same fee as during the period of estimated life expectancy.

PREMIUMS

In most cases, the escrow company pays premiums from funds set aside in a premium reserve account. Who funds the premium account? The viator. Funds are deducted from the purchase price, which reduces the viatical settlement.

Each company withholds an amount equal to premiums expected to come due during life expectancy. Amounts vary, depending on each company's formula.

ALI holds a total of 4 percent of the purchase price for premiums and

---

[a] Page 4, section 11 of the contract.

"other variable ongoing expenses." LifeLine and AMG deduct an amount equal to life expectancy plus one year. The formula is the same for Dedicated Resources, Viatical Benefactors, and Legacy Capital: an amount equal to 1.5 times life expectancy.

How does this work? Take, for example, a viator whose life expectancy is estimated at three years and a policy with annual premiums of $500. LifeLine and AMG would deduct $2,000 (three times $500 plus another $500 for one year). Dedicated Resources, Viatical Benefactors, and Legacy Capital would deduct $2,250 (three times $500 plus $750 for another 1.5 years).

However, if life expectancy is inexact, a range, for example, between 24 and 36 months, the companies could choose 24 months or 36 months. Legacy Capital takes the "midpoint" of these two periods (30 months) and deducts additional premiums for those 6 months—approximately $250, for a total of $2,500. This is what is meant by the company's term, "the midpoint of life expectancy."

PREMIUMS—POSTLIFE EXPECTANCY

What happens if a viator outlives his or her life expectancy and premiums in the reserve account are depleted? Investors must pay premiums. Viatical Benefactors promises to notify investors

> in ample time . . . to meet any premium deadlines.

LifeLine is more specific. This company will contact investors

> in writing 60 days prior to a potential lapse and request additional premium funds . . .[a]

At Legacy Capital,

---

[a] Page 2, section V of the contract.

the investor will be contacted and asked to fund any shortfall in premiums along with related administrative costs.[a]

Dedicated Resources warns investors that if payment is not received within ten days of written demand by certified mail or wire, the company can use "any legal means" to collect such funds, and the investor will be responsible for associated costs.

"Any legal means" sounds a bit nasty. How nasty is it? Not very because the amount in question is likely to be so small that it would be relegated to small claims court. However, such an action could result in a lien against the investor's home or car.

ALI annually collects 4 percent of the death benefit from investors to pay ongoing costs including premiums and loans.[b]

AMG investors don't face continuous and seemingly endless payments in order to keep the policy in force: AMG provides a bank loan to cover payments. You may be told that the bank loan is at AMG's expense. This is true until the policy matures. Then, investors are charged for loan principal and interest at "(3) points above the published prime rate."[c] This is the typical rate charged by banks for business loans.

Investors can't ignore AMG's bill for loan principal or interest. The costs are automatically deducted from policy proceeds by the trustee of the escrow account, who is the sole and irrevocable beneficiary.[d]

One interesting point: No mention is made by AMG of an option for investors who want to save this interest and use pay-as-you-go arrangement.

---

[a] Page 2, number 11 of the contract.

[b] Page 13 of the contract.

[c] Page 2, number 6 of the contract.

[d] Page 1, number 3(d) of the contract. The same terms apply to IRA accounts.

PREMIUM RESERVES

If the viator dies sooner than expected, funds remain in the premium reserve account. What happens to those funds?

AMG admits that it keeps the funds.[a] Other companies may do so, too, but they are silent about this. Some state they *may* apply excess premiums to other policies that exceed life expectancy—but don't count on it. Viatical Benefactors is the only company to commit in writing that it will apply these funds to other policies.[b]

POLICY LOANS

With cash value policies, it's possible that the viator has an outstanding policy loan. Only two contracts mention policy loans.[c] AMG requires policies to be conveyed free of loans, liens, and encumbrances.[d] Loans are paid off before title is transferred, usually from purchase funds.

Legacy Capital handles policy loans in one of two ways:

♦ Loans and estimated future interest are deducted from the death benefit, or

♦ ". . . upon the closing of the Viatical investment" [e]

In effect, the viator pays the loan. Thus, the question is, Which alternative is more favorable to investors?

With the first option, investors purchase a smaller death benefit. This

---

[a] Page 2, number 6 of the contract.

[b] Page 6 of Viatical Benefactors' contract. This company also will apply interest accruing on the premium reserve account to satisfy any overdue maturities.

[c] Legacy Capital's contract is the only one that informs investors that loans reduce death benefits, but it does not provide details.

[d] Page 1, number 3(e) of the AMG's contract.

[e] Page 1, section 1(d) of Legacy's contract. This is one of the rare instances where the contracts of two companies use similar outline style and similar numbers for categories.

should result in a smaller purchase price. It also means if the viator outlives estimated life expectancy, the investor will be required to pay the loan interest. However, if the death benefit is small, it's likely the loan amount will be small and the loan interest negligible.

However, if the loan principal is large, the second alternative may be better for investors. Large loan amounts could mean large loan interest payments. This is likely with older policies where cash values accumulate to the point that a large loan is possible.

POLICY LOAN INTEREST

The same companies that fail to address policy loans don't mention loan interest. If the policy has an existing loan, be sure to clarify with the viatical company how loan interest is handled. Remember to get answers in writing.

CO-OWNERSHIP

Consider this scenario: You co-own a policy with ten strangers. The insured outlives life expectancy. Premiums in the reserve account are depleted. Three of the co-owners don't pay their pro rata share of premiums. What now?

With ALI's unique program, this problem won't occur.[a] Of the remaining companies, only two address the problems of co-ownership.

LifeLine bills co-owners for their pro rata shares. If co-owners don't pay, LifeLine offers these alternatives:

◆ Take loans against policy cash values or dividends
◆ Use excess in reserves from policies of insureds who died prior to depletion of the funds

If neither of these options is available, the policy will lapse. No consideration is given to collecting excess premium from responsible co-owners and returning their pro rata share to them on pay day. It may not be possible for them to do this without changing the contract, since beneficiaries

---

[a] See chapter 10, "Wealthy or Wannabe?" for details about ALI's program.

are entitled to be paid certain percentages with no set-aside for expenses owed in arrears.

AMG's contract tackles this problem head-on.

> Any co-owner who signs this Agreement shall be deemed to be a party hereto and shall be jointly and severally liable with the Purchaser for the obligations of Purchaser hereunder. [a]

Joint and several liability is:

> The liability that exists when a creditor has the option of suing one liable party separately or all liable parties together. Each wrongdoer is individually responsible for the entire judgment, and the person who has been wronged can collect from one wrongdoer or from all of them together until the judgment is satisfied. [5]

Each co-owner has a responsibility but AMG won't bother investors for excess premiums during the course of the investment. Instead, they advance the amount as they do for sole owners—by means of a bank loan. The loan will be repaid with interest from proceeds of the policy.

Other contracts make no mention of co-ownership problems. Don't open yourself to surprises by assuming you know how these problems will be addressed. Ask the viatical company and *get answers in writing.*

OTHER EXPENSES

ALI is the only company whose contract spells out the portion of purchase price that goes to expenses. Although ALI's investment program bears little resemblance to other viatical investments, their company's allocations appear to be typical:

- ♦ 6.25 percent of purchase price for sales commissions
- ♦ 12.2 percent for marketing, office expense, bank and custodial fees, accounting, and other professional fees

---

[a] Page 3, number 19 of the contract.

♦ 4.5 percent as contingency reserve to pay ongoing premiums, as well as any legal or regulatory expenses that may occur. These expenses are covered, in part, through annual fees projected not to exceed 6.33 percent of total death benefits.[a]

Other contracts are not specific about expenses. For example, AMG's contract states nothing more than that the company is

compensated for their services by receiving a portion of the Escrow Deposit tendered by the Investor . . . [b]

LifeLine's contract is silent about operating expenses, as are its marketing materials. But Scott Page, president of Page & Associates and LifeLine, told a reporter that his company takes 15 to 20 percent of purchase price for expenses. This charge may be billed to investors *after* they receive the proceeds of the policy.[6] Alternatively, it may be deducted from the purchase price.[c]

Similar percentages probably apply to most viatical companies. Here's why:

♦ Viatical funding firms pay 6 percent of the death benefit to viatical brokers who bring viators to them.[d]

♦ Commissions ranging from 5 to 9 percent of the purchase price are paid to sales agents who sign up investors.[e]

♦ There are other policy acquisition costs. These include payments for medical records, copying of all data, and the time and effort to obtain these records.

---

[a] Details about this program are in chapter 10, "Wealthy or Wannabe?"

[b] Page 2, number 7 of the contract.

[c] Page 2, section VII-D of the contract. If expenses are deducted from the purchase price, it means you buy a smaller death benefit.

[d] See, Wolk, "Cash for the Final Days," for details.

[e] Source: agent contracts.

The question is, Who pays these fees?

Funding firms allocate certain amounts for policy acquisition costs. Either the companies bear these costs, as when a viator applies to them directly, or they bear them indirectly—by paying the broker who brings the complete file to them. That is why funding firms claim that all viators receive the same net offer, whether they apply directly or through a broker. Thus, when a viatical settlement is financed by an outside investor, the viator will not receive an amount equal to the purchase price but an amount equal to purchase price less these expenses. As Legacy Capital explains in their contract,

> The compensation for the Agent shall be included in the purchase price of the Viatical Investment, and no further payments or fees will be required by the Investor beyond the agreed Viatical Investment, except for future premiums, and future Escrow Agent and/or tracking entity fees . . . . [a]

MEDICAL UNDERWRITING

Medical underwriting is of paramount importance. Yet most companies make short shrift of what they tell investors.[b]

The brochure from Viatical Benefactors—not the contract—informs investors that they will receive a "Life Expectancy Report" prepared for that particular viator. A separate four-page report describes the company that prepares this estimate: American Viatical Services (AVS), the first national firm to specialize in life expectancy estimates.[c]

LifeLine, which also uses the services o f AVS, includes a brief description of the expertise of the staff at AVS. If this is not sufficient, investors willing to travel to LifeLine's Florida headquarters may examine viator records on its

---

[a] Page 2, section 5 of the contract.

[b] To learn what goes on behind the scenes, see chapter 5.

[c] See chapter 6.

premises. Just don't expect the company to show investors everything.[a]

Legacy Capital, in its purchase agreement, says,

> **The Investor has the right to verify any information provided by the Agent in reference to this Viatical Investment.** [b]

Legacy doesn't suggest how this might be verified, nor if the information is limited to name, age, and policy number.

Dedicated Resources openly states that purchasers will not have access to *any* information that identifies viators. According to Michael Zadoff, president of Dedicated Resources, this strict policy was the result of learning that an investor phoned the insurer to find out about a viator. The investor was inadvertently transferred to the office of an executive—the viator. When the secretary answered, "Mr. X's line, Jeannie speaking," the investor demanded to know why Mr. X was at work: "He's supposed to be dying," she told the secretary.

How does a viatical company manage to sell a policy to investors, when investors have no information that allows them to verify information?

"It's not an easy sell," Zadoff admits. "Investors have to trust us and realize that we plan to be in the business for the next two decades, at least."

This is a vision of how the industry should be and hopefully will be, one day. If investors could trust viatical companies, not only would their money be safe but viators' privacy rights and confidentiality would not be sacrificed to profit motives.

---

[a] At the time contracts were reviewed, LifeLine employed American Viatical Services for life expectancy estimates. According to Philip Loy, this no longer is true except in rare cases where a buyer insists on LE reports from AVS. Scott Page of LifeLine confirmed this, addin g that his company now uses practicing physicians with specialities in the various diseases.

[b] From page 4 of Legacy Capital's contract.

INSURANCE UNDERWRITING

Once again, the contract and brochures give short shrift to a vital area—insurance underwriting. For details about little-known areas of insurance risk, see chapters 5, 7, 8, and 9, .

RIGHT TO RESCIND (CANCEL)

If your check sat in escrow for 60 days you may want to cancel your purchase order and invest elsewhere. If it sat in escrow, it's likely the company hasn't enough policies to sell. You might want to cancel your purchase order when you develop "buyer's remorse," which may occur after learning about risks far worse than any disclosed to you by the sales agent. Can you rescind?

ALI makes no mention of a right to rescind. They expect sophisticated investors—people with a net worth of $1 million and $200,000 to invest— to do their homework before investing.

Regarding the other companies, watch for contradictory messages. The contract from Viatical Benefactors grants investors a unilateral right to rescind—for any cause. They promise a full refund less any funds used to complete a viatical settlement transaction.[a] This means if you sent a check for $10,000 with the intention of buying shares of two policies and one policy was viaticated, your refund will be the remaining $5,000 that sits in escrow.

However, in their brochure, Viatical Benefactors says this:

> Once the money is in escrow, you're committed to buying the policy unless the seller fails to meet all the requirements. There is a slim chance that Viatical Benefactors would substitute another investor in your place, but only in an extreme circumstance. You should make your final decision before placing your money with the escrow agent.

LifeLine allows investors a 72-hour recession period from the date of delivery of the closing documents. What does this mean?

---

[a] Page 4, section "three" of the contract from Viatical Benefactors. [sic]

Closing refers to transfer of ownership. Practically speaking, recession should take place prior to this. In order to allow investors 72 hours to change their minds, LifeLine must have investors standing by, waiting to have their funds placed. This makes it easy for them to get a substitute investor.

LifeLine refunds the total investment, less a $750 administrative fee, within 30 days of cancellation notice being delivered to the company.[a]

Dedicated Resources allows a "Right of Recession" only if it is unable to place your funds

within 60 days of execution of the agreement or payment, whichever is later. Reasonable charges may apply. [b]

These charges may be reasonable, but amounts are not specified.

A word about recession fees: A company takes time to process purchase orders, and time to process cancellations. It should be compensated for its time and effort.

Although other companies don't address recession at this time, it's unlikely that any legitimate company will be excessively fussy if an investor cancels before the viator is paid. The newness of the industry coupled with its competitiveness demand good public relations of companies that plan to stay in business.

However, it's another story if the investment is placed with a maverick company. According to a former sales agent who worked for one of these companies, their funds are stored in the Cayman Islands, far beyond the reach of any disgruntled investors.

RISK DISCLOSURE
Most contracts include a paragraph or two in which investors attest to having the sophistication to evaluate the investment or access to professional

---

[a] Page 3, section VI of the contract.

[b] Page 3, "Article Five" of LifeLine's contract.

advisors, or to being suitable for the investment in terms of net worth and able to bear the loss of their entire investment.[7] In other words, investors must proclaim that they are aware of and accept all risks. These are the risks companies tell you about.

LifeLine' brochure mentions—almost breezily—two risks: life expectancy and liquidity, and encourages investors to seek professional advice before making a decision to purchase.

AMG requires investors to sign a disclosure that includes the warning that life expectancy estimates "cannot be construed as a guaranty or warranty of the survival period of any particular individual." To its credit, AMG discloses a number of risks other companies won't whisper about. Chief among these risks:

- There is no established market into which an investor can resell a viatical settlement.
- Medical developments may extend the lives of some individuals with terminal diseases.
- Fraudulent transactions of individuals cannot be completely eliminated by the most scrupulous underwriting.[a]

One item in the list is truly remarkable—the most accurate statement about state guarantee funds offered by any viatical company:

when it makes good on the life insurance policy, [it] may do so only after great delay and possibly not pay full death benefits.

By contrast, Legacy Capital, in its brochure (but not the contract) describes the greatest risk as "the life of the insured himself." In other words, the viator might outlive life expectancy. Legacy also warns that viaticals are not liquid investments.

Viatical Benefactors defines two risk categories: Maturity risk—"the possibility that the viator will outlive the predicted life expectancy," and

---

[a] These are exact quotes.

cancellation risk.

> Cancellation risk is the risk that the investor will have no claim
> or only partial claim to the total death benefit.

In two separate places Dedicated Resources states that this is not a liquid investment and that the investor will not have access to these funds until the demise of the insured. Additionally, Dedicated admits that maturity date cannot be guaranteed, that annual rate of return cannot be determined until the insured's demise, that the viatical settlement is not a product of or guaranteed by any financial institution, and that it

> may be subject to investment risk and possible loss of principal.

ALI devotes two pages of ten-point type to "Risk Factors." Among these risks is governmental regulation—the possibility that viatical investments will become "regulated so as to adversely affect the transaction." [a]

IRA FUNDS
Most viatical companies, including all the legitimate companies, have enlisted a custodial service for investors who wish to use viaticals in their IRAs. This doesn't make it legal. For a complete discussion of issues surrounding IRAs, see chapter 10, "Wealthy or Wannabe?" At this point there are three points to keep in mind:

♦ Investors with self-directed IRAs are completely responsible for their investment decisions.
♦ Read the fine print in the IRA application. Read everything.
♦ Do not turn over custody of your IRA to the sales promoter, its attorney, account, or any of its agent other than a verifiable custodial service. Or, in the words of the National Association of Securities

---

[a] Pages 15-16 of ALI's contract.

Administrators Association (N.A.S.A.A.):

> Never transfer or roll-over your IRA or other retirement funds directly to an investment promoter. Your fund has to go to a pension fund administrator, such as a bank, trust department or mutual fund. If your money is sent directly to the promoter, it is not going into a recognized IRA and, even worse, may be gone for good.

CONFLICTS OF INTEREST

There is a very real possibility that policies sold to investors are those the viatical companies rejected for their own portfolios. It's also likely that they accept policies from some viators solely for the purpose of earning commissions from investors. For these reasons it may be preferable to purchase viatical investments through a stockbroker or licensed insurance agent—a professional who represents several viatical companies as well as other financial products.

Although other financial products don't pay comparably high commissions, licensed financial professionals are obligated to recommend products that suit the individual's needs. Additionally, licensed financial professionals are obligated to perform due diligence for investors.

There are more reasons why this may be the safest way to invest in viaticals. See chapter 11, "Conclusion."

END NOTES

1. In a Cease and Desist Hearing conducted by California's Dept. of Insurance (August 1996), it was revealed that National Medical Funding of San Diego was a front for Life Partners, an illegal viatical company. For details, see chapter 6, *"Cash for the Final Days,* Gloria G. Wolk, Bialkin Books, 1997. See Order Form on last page.

2. List of licensed viatical companies dated October 3, 1997, provided to the author by Sandy Cohill, Secretary Specialist at Florida's Dept. of Insurance.

3. ". . . LPI often appeared as the owner of record of the policies, and not the investors." As the district court noted, "creditors of LPI might be able to reach the policies, were LPI to encounter financial difficulties." Footnote to Judge Patricia Wald's dissent, *SEC v. Life Partners, Inc. and Brian Pardo,* Appellants, No. 95-5364, July 5, 1996.

4. If viatical companies followed the model of banks in setting up CDs, there might be a safer way to arrange for multiple owners. Unfortunately, when the seller or marketing company is owner, purchasers may have nothing. In one recent situation

> the California Department of Corporations filed suit to close 3 Orange County financial brokers for allegedly duping customers—many of them elderly— into investing $26 million in unregistered certificates of deposit.

In some case investors bought fractional interests in CDs, bu t the certificates remained in the broker's name. "The investor has nothing—there's no liquidity, there's nothing in their name," said Bill McDonald, assistant commissioner for the department.

Barbara Marsh, "Investors Duped in CD Scam, State Charges." *The Los Angeles Times,* April 18, 1998.

5. William P. Statsky, *West's Legal Thesaurus/Dictionary,* West Publishing Co., St. Paul, Minnesota, 1986.

6. Amy Ellerson, "Ill Friend was Spark for Insurance Buy-Outs." *The Miami Herald,* March 24, 1997.

7. Some companies ask for a net worth statement in which all assets and debts detailed. These statements and asset declarations are required by SEC regulations for companies that offer private placement securities. At this time this is misleading, this viatical settlements investments are not considered securities.

90

CHAPTER FIVE

❖

FINDING RISK

Here's what experts look for, what they should look for, and some items they are likely to miss.

Investors are told that "strict" underwriting safeguards their investment. Don't be impressed by this, unless you know the answers to these questions:

- ♦ How good are the underwriters (the experts who evaluate the risks)? What is the level of their expertise?
- ♦ What criteria do these experts use?

These are not idle questions. At least two viatical funding firms were forced to go to court when insurers balked at paying death claims. These court battles (see chapters 8 and 9) are closely linked to underwriting—the process of finding and putting a price on risk. Following is what most underwriters look for and why and what they are likely to miss.

MEDICAL UNDERWRITING

Medical underwriting (evaluation) is designed to answer two questions.

- ♦ Legal competency: Is the insured of sound mind and capable of executing this contract?
- ♦ What is the projected life expectancy of the insured?

— Legal Competency —

If the viator is not legally competent, disowned beneficiaries have cause to challenge the sale in court.

What, exactly, is legal competency? For the viatical process, legal competency can best be described as

> **the ability to understand in a general way the nature and extent of the property to be disposed of, one's relationship to those who would naturally claim a substantial benefit from the will, and the practical effect of the will as executed.**[1]

"Practical effect" is no less important than "ability to understand." A client may understand what he/she is doing but be unable to manage a large sum of money. Or the viator may fall victim to a scam or squander and neglect real needs. Such an individual would *not* be considered legally competent.

Prior to 1997, viatical providers didn't accept policies from patients with Alzheimer's or other dementia-causing diseases. The law of supply and demand changed this. Now most funding firms accept these insureds if the sale is handled by someone with power of attorney or by a guardian with authority for the client's financial affairs.[a]

— Mortality Risk —

Everyone who purchases life insurance is evaluated for mortality risk. Insurance underwriters perform this evaluation for insurance companies.

---

[a] The guardian may be a family member, a close friend, or someone appointed by the court.

Their task is to calculate the odds that an applicant might die sooner than most people of the same age and gender. Since insurers lose money if a person dies sooner than predicted, a person whose health is less than standard is charged more ("rated") for the greater risk.

Viatical underwriting is the reverse of insurance underwriting. The same question, *when will this person die,* is asked by viatical companies obviously for the opposite reason. Unlike insurance companies, viatical investors lose money when a person dies *later* than predicted. Thus, a person whose health is worse than others gets a larger viaticum.

Viatical underwriting began in a vacuum. Since there was no precedent for estimating life expectancy other than the methods and information sources of insurance underwriters, viatical underwriters began with those methods. Insurance medical data includes

- The applicant's health statement
- Lab reports

  These reports include urine tests for glucose, protein, blood cells and casts, nicotine and cocaine; blood chemistry profiles, including liver and kidney function tests; tests for total and high-density lipoprotein (HDL) cholesterol; and the AIDS antibody test.

- "Attending Physician's Statement" (APS)

  This is a standard insurance form on which the physician notes blood pressure readings, test results, etc., and any comments that will help clarify "ambiguities. At times this form provides new, unsuspected, relevant and important information."[2]

- Blood and urine tests, and sometimes a full medical exam

  An electrocardiogram may be required for policies with large face amounts or for applicants past a certain age.

- Medical literature

  These are case histories and studies of various treatment approaches.

- "Insured-lives" experience, also known as "mortality studies"[3]
- Medical Information Bureau (MIB) records

Note: Unlike viatical underwriters, insurance underwriters never request full medical records.

By contrast, viatical companies never require a physical exam or tests of bodily fluids. Instead, they depend on the APS and two or three years of medical records from all health providers and facilities.[a] The medical packet for any one individual frequently is several inches thick.

If viatical underwriters use insurance resources, the question is *How accurate are mortality studies?* The answer is not very—not if statistics were based on the records of a single insurer. The largest single insurer can't provide enough data to make results reliable. Instead, data is pooled from many life insurers, then evaluated by experts who are independent of any affiliation with these companies.

> Traditionally, such studies have been joint studies conducted by members of the Society of Actuaries and the American Academy of Insurance Medicine. [4]

These joint studies by impartial evaluators use data from hundreds of thousands of lives within every age range. Thus, mortality studies are efficient for life insurers who price policies based on the results of aggregates—thousands of people of that age, sex, lifestyle, health. However, these studies can't be applied with any degree of accuracy to predicting the life expectancy of a particular individual. The studies don't work for insurance underwriting and they don't work for viatical underwriting. Other methods had to be devised. For details, see chapter 6, "Predicting Life Expectancy."

— Finding Medical Risk: Other Companies —

Every viatical company claims "strict underwriting" but few explain what this is. The companies may tell investors that they employ "experts" or "independent experts" but how can you be certain? One investor attempted

---

[a] For example, hospitals and clinics.

to phone the four medical experts who signed life expectancy reports. Using the phone numbers on their letterhead, he reached a fax, a boarding house where the doctor had stayed briefly and left no forwarding information, and dead ends. Further checking revealed that none of these "experts" were members of the state medical association.

In another instance the investigation conducted by the Securities and Exchange Commission revealed that the expert medical consultant employed by unlicensed Life Partners, Inc., was Dr. John Kelly, a physician who had no previous experience treating infectious diseases.[a] Purchases based on Dr. Kelly's life expectancy estimates led clients of one Midwestern investment advisor to lose more than $80 million.[b]

Recently, the beleaguered investment advisor sought a second opinion on several of Dr. Kelly's predictions. He turned to American Viatical Services (AVS), the first national company to specialize in life expectancy estimates.

AVS was unable to make any determination of life expectancy. As Philip Loy, president of AVS, explained,

> Obviously, their doctor had a lot more information when they generated the report. The report was designed not to provide substantive information to investors.

Another problem with finding medical risk is the viatical company that sells a 4-year or 3-year life expectancy as one-year. Since investors usually receive nothing more than a summary report with a life expectancy estimate, how can anyone know if the summary is based on data that would lead other consultants to similar conclusions about life expectancy?

An example of this type of discrepancy can be found in appendix VII, "Cease and Desist." The summary report given to investors describes a viator who had opportunistic infections. When the same medical data were reviewed

---

[a] The SEC also revealed that Dr. Kelly was a shareholder in the viatical company.

[b] As told to the author by one of the principals.

by American Viatical Services, it was found that the viator never had any opportunistic infections.

— Finding Medical Risk: Selected Companies —

A copy of the group insurance guidelines used by underwriters at Accelerated Benefits Capital is in appendix II.[a] Compare this document with the information you receive from companies eager to sell policies to investors. Although other viatical companies may be as thorough as Accelerated Benefits Capital, the information they provide is too limited to come to this conclusion that they are as thorough. Here are a few examples from other companies.

ALI describes medical underwriting in this way:[b]

> reviewing physicians assess a prospective viator's life expectancy within probability parameters of no less than 80% certainty. Policies insuring prospective viators for whom probability is less than 80% will not be purchased. An insured with a six-month life expectancy with 80% certainty might receive a different settlement offer equivalent to an offer given to an insured with a nine-month life expectancy. However, an insured with a six-month life expectancy with 95% certainty will receive a higher settlement offer, consistent with settlements offered to other insureds with life expectancies of six months.

This statement may seem like gobbledy-gook, but you'll get a better understanding after reading Philip Loy's explanation of confidence levels and life expectancy predictions (chapter 6). Then you'll see that the problem with this description is not what it says but what it fails to tell investors. For example, consultants are "physicians who are experienced diagnosticians." Their duties are to "review each prospective viator's medical records." No individual physician or medical group is named.

---

[a] Accelerated Benefits Capital is a licensed funding firm that buys for its own portfolio and does not offer investments to the public.

[b] Page 37 of the prospectus.

At Dedicated Resources, underwriting is turned over to

> an independent physician with expertise in the terminall [sic] illness [who] confirms the diagnosis.

According to Dedicated Resources' brochure (not their contract) their independent physician, Dr. Lon Baratz, is head of Brighton Medicine Associates, an infectious disease specialty firm based in Rochester, New York. Further,

> Dr. Baratz and BMA have handled thousands of terminally ill patients.

Upon what data do experts for Dedicated Resources base their life expectancy estimates? The brochure states

> the viator's extensive lab reports, medical records, history of medication use and reaction to those medications.

Compare this with AMG's description:

> AMG physicians are obtained from the same group of qualified professionals responsible for the original medical underwriting of our corporate affiliate.[a]

In a separate document, AMG explains that records are reviewed by

> a third party Reviewing Physician to determine the viator's general medical condition and life expectancy prognosis. At the same time, the viator's attending physician is asked to complete a required statement verifying that the viator is of sound mind and able to enter willingly into a legal contract.

Legacy Capital similarly follows procedures established by the parent company, Legacy Benefits. An in-house medical staff performs initial

---

[a] AMG's corporate affiliate, Neuma, is a licensed viatical funding firm.

evaluations and prepares a chart to show the clinical events, lab results, medications, etc. This process Eliav said,

> eliminates the people that are not qualified. The charts of people who are qualified then go to specialists, along with the full medical records for 2 or 3 years. These specialists use the charts to save time in going through the entire medical file.

From the brochure that accompanies Legacy Capital's contract:

> a medical opinion is prepared by an independent board-certified physician who uses medical and statistical data to create the most safe and judicious life expectancy estimate possible.

LifeLine, which contracts out medical underwriting to American Viatical Services (AVS), provides investors with a three-paragraph description of AVS which includes the following information:

> several different scientific disciplines affording us the wide variety of knowledge and experience to perform accurate medical reviews. The professional medical specialties include Infectious Disease, Oncology, Cardiology, Ophthalmology and Homeopathy. Other areas of expertise include Immunology, Microbiology and Biophysics.[a]

Viatical Benefactors, another client of AVS, provides investors with a five-page summary of the medical evaluation process. Aaron Kokol of Viatical Benefactors explained some of what he learned from working with American Viatical Services:

> Some companies call life expectancy at one to two years, when it's possible the viator will live ten years. We want to know the patient's experience with protease inhibitors. If he has 100 T-cells and hasn't taken protease yet he has a lot of options, and probably is a long-term survivor. Decline is more predictable, if a viator went from one protease inhibitor to another. If comparable drugs failed

---

[a] Other companies may use evaluation methods as efficient as those of AVS, but they fail to communicate this to investors.

to boost the viator, his medical options are running out.[a]

At times a viatical company may ask medical consultants for a life expectancy estimate with a 50 percent probability. In other words, they want experts to convert an estimate of five years (with an 80 percent probability) into two years (with a 50 percent probability) because a two year estimate is easy to sell.

— Companies Ignore Consultants —

Stringent underwriting may not be reflected in the purchase price if the company ignores consultants' reports. This is what happened to Dignity Partners.

Underwriters warned Dignity Partners that new AIDS drugs seemed to have potential to prolong the lives of patients. Thus, the experts turned in life expectancy estimates of three to five years for a series of viators who, six months earlier, would have had life expectancies of one year. The principals at Dignity Partners resisted this news.

"We can't go to the table with this," they told the consultants. "Prices will be too low and viators won't accept our offers. If we don't pay more, we'll lose sales to the competition."[b]

And Dignity made competitive bids and they acquired policies. And when they went broke and had to liquidate their portfolio, it was at a loss of $3 million.[c]

This happened to a funding firm that was renown for its strict underwriting, a firm that risked its own dollars. What happens in viatical firms whose profits come solely from fees?

---

[a] Via telephone conversation.

[b] This is as close to a true version of what happened as one can get, based on Dignity's SEC filings.

[c] For details, see Chapter 8: "Fraud Watch."

INSURANCE UNDERWRITING

The first concern of viatical firms is the rating of the insurance company that issued the policy. These ratings reflect insurers' claims-paying ability and overall solvency. Most investors take comfort if the policy is backed by a household name like Metropolitan or Prudential, but what about Lincoln National? UNUM? Modern Woodmen of America? Each of these companies is top-rated ("A+") as judged by independent rating services. Then there's Utica Life, Jefferson-Pilot, and many others whose names are unfamiliar to most people. Roughly 2,000 U.S. companies specialize in life insurance.[a]

With so many insurers, how is it possible to know if the company that issued the policy is financially solvent? All viatical companies claim to accept policies from companies rated are no lower than a certain level, as rated by an independent rating service such as A.M. Best, Standard & Poor's, or Moody's.[b]

What about an insurer that is rated "B+"?[c] Avoid it. Some companies do accept policies with low ratings, aware that investors have no notion what it means. (Never mind what it means. Just remember: Avoid ratings lower than "A." And read chapter 7, "Belly-up Insurance.")

Are these ratings fool-proof? No. By the time they get into print, ratings may be a year old.[d] Then, too, the viatical company may not have used the most current rating. What should do you do?

First, ask for a photocopy of the evaluation by the rating service. Then check for yourself. Hire an expert to provide a current solvency report in everyday language. The small fee for this report could save you thousands (and

---

[a] This figure does not take into the account the many property/casualty insurers that offer life insurance to clients.

[b] These ratings can generally be checked in public libraries. Be sure to check the *latest updates.* You may not have been told the truth.

[c] LifeLine accepts B+ policies, according to information on their web site. See appendix III.

[d] The year before Executive Life went "belly-up" it was rated "A."

spare you many sleepless nights).[a]

Why don't viatical companies order current solvency reports and provide them to investors? It's possible they're not aware that such reports exist. Or they are not aware that state insurance guarantee funds do not offer the guarantees they claim. The following, from Dedicated Resources, is typical of statements made by nearly every viatical company:

> **As an added safety measure, generally State Guarantee Insurance Funds assure payments to beneficiaries of up to $300,000.***

The asterisk at the end of that statement leads to a clarification in tiny print: "Guarantees vary by state." To understand what this statement means, see chapter 7.

The concept of a state guarantee fund is that all insurers licensed to market a particular type of policy within that state must stand ready to make good on the claims of an insurer that becomes insolvent. This sounds good but is not good enough, for several reasons:

♦ The guarantee fund is an outline, nothing more than a plan to be implemented when a need arises. In reality, no fund exists until insurers are assessed for contributions for a particular situation. Before an assessment is made the failing insurer must get a court determination of insolvency (e.g., bankruptcy). This doesn't happen quickly.

♦ Once insolvency is declared by a bankruptcy court, other insurers are called in. Then, and not until then, are they required to come up with a payment plan.

♦ This, too, means a wait. How long is anyone's guess.

Before you rely on your state's guarantee fund to protect your investment, check the wording of your state's guarantee fund law. You may not be

---

[a] See chapter 7, "Belly-up Insurance."

covered. In some states and under certain conditions, investor-beneficiaries don't have standing to make a claim. In Ohio, for example, you won't have a *"covered claim"* if, on the date of the occurrence giving rise to the claim (the insolvency), your net worth is greater than the amount allowed by the guarantee fund.

If you are covered by the state fund, you certainly won't be covered dollar-for-dollar. To understand the dollars and sense of this statement, be sure to read chapter 7, "Belly-up Insurance." Then you'll know why it's important to verify that the insurer not only is "A" rated or higher but is solvent as of the day you sign that check.

Rarely are other risks mentioned by most viatical companies. Not one viatical company tells investors that viatical sales are prohibited in some locales. Of course, it's possible the companies don't know this. But where such sales are prohibited, the transaction is not valid. This means named beneficiaries can challenge your right to insurance proceeds. It's even possible that policy ownership will revert to the insured—and the insured may not be required to return the viaticum. For details, see chapter 9, "Fraud Watch."

Most of the risks cited above are not commonly known. Following are more common risks, which underwriters should price accordingly.

— Policy Type —

There are two basic types of life insurance: term and permanent (cash value) insurance. Permanent insurance, also known as cash value or whole life, is relatively expensive. Currently, there are a variety of permanent/cash value policies, each with its own set of bells and whistles and new names to match these features (e.g., Universal Life and Variable Life).

Term insurance, while commonly associated with group plans, is available for individual purchase as well. Most term insurance sold today is renewal term, with re-entry provisions. Initial premiums are very low but premiums in later years can be very steep. The low early-years premiums reflect the fact that insurers carry little risk with term policies since these rarely are kept long enough to pay death benefits. Term insurance is designed for temporary, or short-term needs. When the need no longer exists, insureds either lapse their policies, switch to another company's new term rates, or convert the term plan to permanent insurance.

However, if an insured wants to continue a term policy, at the end of the term period (usually five or 10 years) the insured must "re-enter." In order to re-enter at a low rate, the insured must be medically underwritten. If the insured is not healthy, the policy can be renewed—but at the maximum premium rate. This rate may be 30 times higher than the premium that was paid in the previous term period. Keep this in mind if sales agents tell you that premiums for this million dollar term policy are $500 a year. You might find yourself billed for premiums of $15,000 a year.

The greatest problems for investors occur with group insurance. An investor can buy the death benefits but can't take ownership of the policy. The reason is that the insureds themselves don't own a policy. A group trust (e.g., the employer or association) owns the master policy. Individuals are insured through this master policy, and receive a certificate as evidence that they are covered. Here's what Legacy Capital tells investors about group insurance:

> If the policy purchased is part of a group policy, and the group policy is terminated, the coverage will have to be converted to an individual policy. Adequate procedure will be initiated by the Escrow Agent to convert that policy to an individual one. However, in many cases, if the insured is on disability when the group policy is terminated, the coverage will continue without the payment of additional premium as long as the insured's disability continues.[a]

Although industry insiders estimate that between 35 and 40 percent of viatical companies buy group policies, none of the other companies discloses whether they do. If group policies are resold to investors, investors should know the risks they may incur. See appendix II.

---

[a] Page 1 of Legacy Capital's "Disclosure of Benefits and Risk Factors."

— Age of the Policy—

Any policy must be older than two years. The reason for this is to assure the policy is past the two-year contestability period. And yet this may not be true, if the insured allowed the policy to lapse and then had it reinstated. Details follow.

— Incontestability Clause —

This clause, which is mandated by state law, prevents insurers from contesting (voiding) a life insurance policy after the contestability period (usually two years). In many states this provision is all-embracing; insurers lose the right to cancel the policy, even for cause. But this isn't true in all states. Here's what happened in Michigan, where state law allows fraud ("material misrepresentation") to supercede incontestability:

> In the 1960's a man took out a policy with Prudential, naming his wife as beneficiary. Several years later he died by accident. Prudential discovered that two weeks prior to applying for the policy the man consulted a doctor about something, but he didn't state the doctor visit on the application. Although the man didn't suffer from any health condition, the court ruled this was 'material misrepresentation,' and voided the policy. [a]

— Lapses and Reinstatements —

A policy will lapse when premiums are not paid past the grace period. Reinstatement requires the insured to make payment of back premiums and sign a statement of good health. If the policy lapsed and was reinstated, the two-year contestability period begins anew.

— Assignment —

---

[a] As told to the author by Robert Shear, president of Viatical Association of America and president of funding firm, Accelerated Benefits Capital. Michigan officials confirmed that fraud supersedes the contestability clause.

Assignment means ownership may be transferred to another party. Assignment may be a serious problem with group policies. It's not unusual for the master policy to prohibit transfer of ownership. More on this can be found in appendices II and III.

— Beneficiaries —

The viator's beneficiaries must sign a release to relinquish any claim to future rights to the policy. However, in some states if a viator has dependent children, the viator may not sell more than 50 percent of the policy. Other problems with beneficiaries include the following:

♦ If there are irrevocable beneficiaries, can they be located so as to get their signed waiver of rights?

♦ Some viators want to keep a portion of death benefits for their loved ones.

♦ Some employee group policies don't allow assignment (transfer of ownership).

♦ Some employee group policies don't allow the insured to name a beneficiary who isn't a family member.

— Fraud —

Most viatical companies don't look for fraud in the insurance application. They should. Fraud occurs when an insured was diagnosed and/or treated before applying for insurance but failed to disclose this on the application. It also occurs if the policy lapsed and was reinstated, but the insured didn't disclose a health problem on the reinstatement form.

New fraud risks are continually coming to light. For details, see chapters 8 and 9.

— Suicide Clause —

If the insured commits suicide during the contestability period, the insurer won't pay. Once past that two-year period, insurers must pay. However, there is cause for concern. The suicide clause could be reactivated past the two-year period if it was a group policy that was converted, or if the policy lapsed and was reinstated.

— Decreasing Face Value —

Decreasing death benefits may occur upon conversion from group policies and with some individually owned policies as well. Mortgage insurance is one example. In such policies death benefits decrease as the mortgage loan is paid off.

— Increasing Face Value —

One way death benefits increase is through a rider known as "Guaranteed Insurability Option." This rider allows the policy owner to increase the death benefit without a requirement for the insured to prove good health. Exercising this rider, which increases the death benefit, will increase premiums, but it's worth the added cost.

Another rider, "Accidental Death and Dismemberment" (AD&D) pays additional benefits if the insured dies by accident.[a]

If death benefits increase, they are assets for which the viator should be paid extra. If the viatical company overlooks this asset or trumpets it to sell a larger death benefit without compensating the viator, beware. A company that cheats terminally ill people is not to be trusted with your investment dollars.

— Policies Insuring Healthy Elderly —

An increasing number of viatical companies now buy policies from healthy elderly (males aged 65 and over; females aged 70 and over). These policies, also known as Senior Settlements, hold great risk for investors. Actuaries have determined that a healthy person of 70 years has a life expectancy of 15 years.

---

[a] AD&D is commonly known as "Double Indemnity," although it doesn't necessarily double the death benefit.

What if the viator lives much longer? Several viatical companies who explored this aspect of investing report that the return is likely to be four percent, at best, after paying premiums for these policies.

— Organ Disease and Donor Lists —

Lastly, viatical companies should ask potential viators who are diagnosed with heart, liver, or kidney disease if they applied to be on any donor lists for organ transplants. To be absolutely certain, underwriters should check donor lists. One viatical company purchased a policy from a 65 year old man who was dying of heart disease. The following year this man was spending most of his time on the golf course, playing golf with the heart of a 27 year old.[a]

---

[a] It's possible that the viatical settlement paid for this man's new life, since organ transplants are very expensive and often not covered by health insurance.

END NOTES

1. William P. Statsky, *West's Legal Thesaurus/Dictionary*. West Publishing Co., St. Paul, Minnesota, 1985.

2. Donald C. Chambers, M.D., *What the General Public Should Know about the Value of Medical Underwriting*. Testimony delivered to the Ohio House of Reps. March 4, 1993. Dr. Chambers is Senior Vice President and Chief Medical Director, Lincoln National Life, and Managing Editor of Lincoln Medical Resource. Available: http://www.lnrc.com/ep/ep_wp1.htm.

3. Insured-lives experience (mortality studies) are statistics gathered over many years from tens of thousands of people. This is what insurance companies refer to when they use the term "aggregates."

4. Chambers, *Ibid.*

CHAPTER SIX

◆

PREDICTING
LIFE EXPECTANCY

Philip Loy

The president of American Viatical Services, the first national
company to specialize in life expectancy estimates and viator
tracking, explains the various methods used for each of these
services and the problems that may arise.

Life expectancy evaluations are used by viatical settlement
companies to determine the discount paid for life insurance. While
there are no minimum requirements for information used to produce an
evaluation, most individuals or companies agree that a review of the medical

records should include
- ♦ At least two years of attending physician's chart notes
- ♦ Laboratory data
- ♦ Radiological reports
- ♦ Consulting specialists' reports

Some medical evaluations include a discussion with the potential viator's attending physician. These discussions can be pivotal in determining life expectancy evaluation, since it is rare that a medical record contains 100 percent of the data required for an evaluation. Attending physician discussions also provide the reviewer an opportunity to discover any fraudulent data in the medical records.

The following briefly describes various methods of evaluating life expectancy.

CLINICAL EVALUATION

This evaluation is performed by physicians with a specialty in the disease (e.g., an infectious disease specialist for a patient whose terminal illness is AIDS). Remaining life expectancy is determined by a review of existing medical records, including laboratory reports, and the physician's own medical experience.

This type of determination typically does not incorporate the most current research on the disease or future medications. As a result, these evaluations usually *understate* life expectancy and the viator usually outlives the evaluation.

STATISTICAL EVALUATION

Companies that use this approach rely on the fact that there is an average life expectancy for each disease category. However, since statistical data is based on the "law of large numbers," it is not applicable to any one individual. And advances in medical science outpace statistical databases. These two factors make these databases all but obsolete. Thus, the statistical approach usually understates life expectancy.

As an example, statistically no more than 50 percent of patients with adenocarcinoma of the pancreas survive six months, and only 1 or 2 percent survive three years. Based solely on the statistical approach, it would be safe to provide an evaluation of one year for this type of patient.

This disease came to our attention when our company was asked to re-evaluate five viators whose policies were sold to individual investors. Purchase prices, based on the statistical approach, resulted in life expectancies of less than six months.

But these viators had already survived beyond the statistical norm. As a result, our evaluations also went beyond statistical factors. The results of our evaluation showed that *only one of the five* investors had paid a reasonable amount for the policy.

MULTI-DISCIPLINARY APPROACH

The multi-disciplinary approach incorporates the collective knowledge of several different specialties, statistical data, investigational studies, information on investigational new drugs (INDs), and finally, a discussion with the attending physician for each potential viator.

Regarding INDs, new medications and treatments are included in this approach even before they are approved by the F.D.A.[a] This is important because patients will be eligible for new treatments either during clinical trials of new drugs or immediately after FDA approval.

This approach generally is *accurate* or *overstates* life expectancy.

DETERMINE WHICH APPROACH IS USED

To determine which approach is used by a company, ask for the source of the medical evaluation as well as for an explanation of the *method* of evaluation. A viatical company that markets to investors should be willing to disclose the credentials and experience of the individual or company providing an

---

[a] Food and Drug Administration.

evaluation.

Many viatical companies retain their own physician. These physicians may even be board members of the viatical settlement company. It is of utmost importance that the company or individual providing an evaluation be a true third party to the transaction with no direct ties to any one company. Obviously, a company or physician who provides evaluations to several companies is preferable since that individual will not show bias in favor of any one viatical company's bottom line.

QUALIFIED EVALUATORS

The "track record" of the evaluator (company or individual) is the best determining factor. Don't be afraid to ask about the experience of the company or individual. Make sure this experience spans several years and that data matches what you are buying.

As an example, if you are buying policies with a 36-month life expectancy, has the evaluator had sufficient experience at that life expectancy? In other words, if the evaluator has only done life expectancies of a few months or less, he/she has no experience determining life expectancies of 24 months and beyond.

CONFIDENCE LEVELS

For our company, confidence level does not mean that we are more (or less) confident that the person will die at the predicted time. We define confidence level as

the ability to sufficiently understand the medical condition of the patient in order to provide an evaluation.

In other words, we need sufficient data to understand the treatment rationale of the attending physician and his/her willingness to incorporate new medical therapies as they become available.

Since we seldom receive a complete file for our purpose of determining life expectancy, the confidence level also incorporates missing pieces filled in through our discussion with the attending physician. In a sense, it is our comfort level with our evaluation.

Some companies use confidence levels to achieve shorter life expectancies. They rationalize that life expectancy is a continuum, with only the confidence changing. In some sense this is true. But it is incorrect to assume that an individual with an 80 to 90 percent chance of living 36 months has a 50 percent chance of living 12 months. This is simply a mathematical ploy to *make the evaluation fit what an investor will pay.* In this example, barring an unpredictable accident, the chance of a person dying in 12 months is very small.

We do provide evaluations as low as 70 percent confidence for some clients but always accompanied by a companion life expectancy at 90 percent confidence. An individual or company unable to commit to that higher level of confidence shouldn't be providing an evaluation. Such a viatical company is probably more interested in just getting your money.

For practical purposes, never accept an evaluation with less than 89 percent confidence *unless* you know what the life expectancy is at the higher confidence level.

POINT OF VIEW DIFFERENCES

Understanding and treating a disease leads to one point of view. Determining life expectancy of a person never seen by the evaluating physician leads to another point of view.

A treating physician's point of view is always "life." When asked, "How long will this person live?" most physicians answer optimistically, albeit with some level of confidence. This is not adequate for investors who purchase a policy based on life expectancy—an approximate date for the patient's demise.

CHANGING PROCEDURES FOR VIATICAL EVALUATIONS

The evaluation process *must* change to keep pace with advancing medical treatment. For example, prior to mid-1995 some evaluations provided by our company were "too short." At the time we could not include protease inhibitors and combination therapy in evaluations of AIDS patients. There was not enough data to justify these changes. We began to include protease inhibitors and combination therapy in mid-1995, which was a dramatic departure from standard evaluations done by competitors. Another six months would pass before the first protease inhibitor was approved and nearly one year before combination therapy was universally accepted.

These revised procedures resulted in longer life expectancy estimates, and clients complained that estimates were "too long." Longer life expectancies meant they couldn't buy those policies, and we lost almost all our clients. A few clients who believed we were on the right track stayed with us but bought fewer policies.

Then, in April 1996, the viatical industry was rocked by the Vancouver AIDS Conference.[b] Many viatical companies and investors stopped buying AIDS policies, believing that AIDS patients would live forever or at least too long for viatical investments to be profitable. These new medications should change evaluation procedures, but they do not make AIDS either a non-terminal disease or nonpredictable disease.

The lesson to be learned is that individuals and companies who provide viatical evaluations should invest significant time in investigation of new treatments and especially INDs.

If a patient has a life expectancy of one year and a major new drug will become available in six months, any evaluation of this patient should incorporate that investigational drug—even if the patient and his/her physician never heard of the drug. They will!

Terminally ill patients seek out every possible method that offers the

---

[b] Ed. note: At the Vancouver Conference research scientists released the news that successful trials of an experimental drug called protease inhibitors, when used in combination with two older drugs, had potential to wipe out all trace of HIV. It was not expected to be a cure, but it meant a longer life span for many AIDS patients.

chance of extending their lives. They enroll in investigational study programs and when there is no other means to finance treatment, use the money provided in a viatical settlement to buy the treatment they seek.

Evaluation procedures must change if they are to keep pace with progressing medical treatment. This is even more important with longer life expectancies. In a sense, the terminally ill patient lives for new treatments that could extend his/her life. These new treatments usually don't change an individual from terminal to non-terminal, but they may extend his/her life for a period of time.

RELIABILITY OF PREDICTIONS

Predictions are more accurate when based on the patient's response to available therapy. Unless you are a gambler, you shouldn't rely on pure statistical data to make your decision because statistics don't factor in a patient's individual responses to therapy or the will to live.

While most terminal diseases have a point in time at which they become very predictable, in general the toughest disease to evaluate is heart disease. The patient frequently considers himself/herself to be terminal, and treating physicians provide documentation to support this belief.

For example, if asked how long a patient may live, the physician will answer, "Six months." This is a typical answer, and the physician probably gave this same answer when the patient was first diagnosed five years earlier.

In other words, no one would be surprised if the patient died within six months—or lived six years. With diseases like heart disease the actual event of dying is sometimes just not predictable.

Although certain individuals with heart disease have very predictable life expectancies, most die from a "cardiac accident" that was not predicted. The accident may take years to develop. Can you afford to wait years for your investment to mature?

Viatical brokers and viatical funding companies do not want to hear that a patient is "not predictably terminal." They can't market a life insurance policy with this prognosis. While a disease that is not predictably terminal may create a sizable return, it also could become a nightmare that investors live with for many years.

ONE- AND FIVE-YEAR LIFE EXPECTANCIES

A life expectancy under 30 months is considered a short evaluation. Most short evaluations are based on actual progression of the patient's disease, including responses to therapy. Evaluations longer than 30 months combine statistical data, new drug advances, and the patient's general response to therapy.

Our company tends to be conservative and feels comfortable with both types of evaluation. In some respects the longer evaluation may be a slighter better "buy" because we try to anticipate new treatments that might be used by the patient's physician. We do this without knowing if the newer therapies will actually be used.

Some companies provide a slightly different approach to the evaluation process for longer life expectancies. These companies provider a shorter (or lower) life expectancy at a lower confidence level, and a longer life expectancy at a higher confidence level.

When the confidence level drops below a certain point, the estimation becomes a trick played on investors. These companies believe life expectancy to be longer but use a low confidence level to sell lower life expectancies to investors. As a result, the viator gets more money, the viatical settlement company gets a better chance of being financially successful, but investors may pay too much for a policy insuring a viator who lives longer than the evaluation.

CHANGES IN LIFE EXPECTANCY

Life expectancy can change. It may not happen often, but it does happen. For instance, at the time of our evaluation, some individuals might be noncompliant with medications. They may refuse them, or they may not take medications according to schedule or required dosage. But they might become compliant after they receive a scare from an opportunistic infection or see a dramatic drop in their T-cells. Then there are people who are compliant but become less so after years of living with a terminal disease. Other times, the change is due to additional data.

It is difficult to be 100 percent accurate when predicting an individual's response to medications yet to be tried. Predictions are based on average response data. As you might guess, not everyone is average. Thus, when actual clinical responses are added the following year, life expectancy may change from the "average" calculation.

This is not to say that it is impossible to predict future life expectancies but rather to emphasize that the more actual data, the better the evaluation.

MEDICAL SITUATIONS TO AVOID

There are situations for any disease in which the disease process is considered chronic but non-terminal. Although it is not common to die of the common cold, it happens. It is not common for an individual with a textbook definition of AIDS to live for 20 years, but it happens.

In the early stage of many diseases, determining life expectancy is nothing more than applying statistics for that disease. Because of this, it is wise to avoid patients who have been recently diagnosed with any disease. However, there are exceptions, such as some very aggressive forms of cancer.

AUTHENTICITY OF MEDICAL RECORDS

Our company sees approximately 1 to 5 percent fraudulent medical records. These may be slight changes that affect life expectancy by a few months or major changes that result in a difference of four or five years. In the worst case, an individual who does not have a terminal illness appears to be terminal. The number of these cases is likely to rise since the reward is great and there is little risk if the fraud is exposed.

Modification or creation of medical records not only is possible but relatively simple in this age of computers with scanners, of advanced document-processing programs, and of modernized physician offices where handwritten charts have been replaced with computerized files.

That is why we place a phone call to every attending physician. Most phone calls take no longer than five minutes. The primary purpose is to discuss pertinent aspects of the file, but this discussion may also reveal whether data is authentic or fake.

After more than three years of calling physicians we have the largest database in the country of treating physicians, for use in viatical settlements.

Since the risk of fraudulent medical records falls on investors, it is prudent for the investor to ask each viatical settlement company *how authenticity of medical records is assured.*

THE TRACKING PROCESS

Tracking, or monitoring, is a service that notifies the investor or viatical settlement company about the medical condition and death of the viator. A variety of methods is used. Among the most popular

  ♦ Postcards from the viator
  ♦ Monthly, quarterly, semiannual, or annual contacts with the viator
  ♦ Monthly, quarterly, semiannual, or annual contacts with the physician
  ♦ Quarterly, semiannual, or annual searches of Social Security numbers

Tracking may be the most important determinant of whether an investor gets paid. If an individual disappears, you will not be able to process a death certificate. This means you don't have an investment.

Also, the tracking process works only with the agreement of the viator. If the viator decides to make tracking difficult, tracking can become impossible. Death may not be known for a year or more after the event— if ever.

The tracking process begins at the time of escrow, when the viator agrees to cooperate. To be effective, the investor or the viatical settlement company must notify the viator that this process is *required* as part of the viatical settlement, and will be required until the viator dies.

Viators are more cooperative when they are allowed to choose from a list of tracking methods equally acceptable to investors. It is much easier to track an individual when he/she knows about and agrees to the method.

Our company, which provides tracking services for companies and individual investors, provides monthly contact with individuals whose life expectancies are less than 12 months, and semi-monthly for individuals with life expectancies of less than 12 months.

These should be minimum guidelines. Contact more than two months apart allows a "trail" to get cold if a viator relocates. At the same time, too frequent contact is a nuisance and infringes on the dignity of the individual with a terminal illness.

TRACKING METHODS

No one method is markedly better than others, but tracking done through the Social Security system is the slowest because of its delay of data input. Despite claims to the contrary, it frequently takes two or three months to input death data into that system. There also are numerous reports of individuals whose data never were input. Additionally, most companies that process searches of the Social Security database do so on a quarterly basis. It is possible for an individual to die six to nine months before the Social Security database can be used to make a claim.

A WORD OF CAUTION

If you wish to use a viator's physician for the purpose of tracking make sure the viator has notified the attending physician of this process, and is assured the physician or office manager is supportive. Some physicians do not believe in viatical settlements and will not cooperate *even with the patient's permission.*

Ed. note: Several viatical companies falsely claim to have life expectancy reports prepared by American Viatical Services. Check to see if the report is on AVS stationery. Investors who have doubts are encouraged to phone AVS.

CHAPTER SEVEN

❖

"BELLY-UP" INSURANCE

Jack W. Traylor, D.P.A.

Investors are told that their principal is guaranteed by insurance companies, and if the insurer goes "belly-up," state guarantee funds will pay. Now for the facts, from someone whose professional experience includes assisting state insurance departments with the resolution of insurer insolvencies.

WHILE DRIVING TO WORK RECENTLY I LISTENED TO A NATIONAL radio call-in program. An insurance expert took a call from a man who asked, "What happens if my annuity company goes `belly-up?'"

The expert gave a professional-sounding answer with references to bankruptcy and the SEC. Her answer seemed to satisfy the caller but was not even close to being correct.

So what does this mean to the man who worries about his insurance company going "belly-up?" It means he must depend on his state government, usually the state insurance department, to take action on any insurance company impairment or insolvency.

If state regulators find an insurance company is financially impaired or insolvent, or simply that continued operation is a danger to the public, regulators are required to seize physical control of the company. After seizure, the state must correct the company's financial problems or close the company.

If the caller had known this, he might have asked, "How does closing down my insurance company help me?" This is a question that regulators are sometimes hard-pressed to answer. From an overall perspective, the public is clearly protected when the state takes over an insolvent company and prevents it from selling additional insurance. But does this action protect current policy holders?

In a state takeover, insurance company management is routinely replaced. Remember, it was this management that caused or, at the very least, failed to prevent the insolvency. In fact, it is not uncommon for the state to file civil (R.I.C.O.) actions against the officers and directors of such a company.[a]

A state takeover replaces management with an independent third party whose duty is to protect the interests of policy holders *before* those of pre-existing trade creditors.[1] Although the law in every state specifies that policy holders must be paid 100 percent before any payment can go to trade creditors, some new creditors are paid before policyholders.[2]

If the radio caller had heard the above, he might have wondered how individual states could coordinate the affairs of a large company operating in many states. There was a time when they did not. In the not-too-distant past,

---

[a] R.I.C.O. = Racketeer Influenced and Corrupt Organizations. This is an anti-racketeering law.

the state where the company was incorporated (the domiciliary state) would attempt to take over the company and work with or around the laws in the other states.

To further complicate matters, each state had its own set of laws and seldom did they match. Multi-state insolvencies were, more often than not, a legal shoot-out between states as each tried to capture assets for their policy holders. Confusion and legal standoff were the order of the day.

Encouraged by a perceived threat of federal action to take back the regulation of insurance, state insurance commissioners and their senior staff began to draft model legislation at the quarterly meetings of the National Association of Insurance Commissioners (N.A.I.C.). They drafted what became known as the Insurers Rehabilitation and Liquidation Model Act.

Fearing Federal regulation more than they did state regulation, the insurance industry joined the task and today a version of the "Model Rehabilitation and Liquidation Act" has been passed in every state.

Of equal importance was the creation of two model guaranty fund acts. One exists for property/casualty companies and another for life/health/annuity companies.

Each state has its own guaranty fund, and often separate funds for property/casualty and life/health/annuity companies. Because of complications that developed when the guaranty funds in each state tried to act independently of each other, a national association was created for each type of fund.

In practice, the national association works with the domiciliary state regulator to administer a multi-state insolvency. While the acts provide for state administrative action against companies, most state regulators prefer to take action through a state court. As a result, in a multi-state insolvency, regulators in the domiciliary state file an action in that state's court. Then, under supervision of the court, together with the national guaranty fund association, they work out a plan of rehabilitation or liquidation that is in the best interest of policy holders.

The model act is quite detailed and provides protections and restrictions on most all aspects of rehabilitation or liquidation. To get to the heart of the question of companies that go bankrupt, we have to turn our attention to a closer look at the guaranty fund system.

LIFE, HEALTH, AND ANNUITY GUARANTY FUND OPERATION

Each state now has a life, health, and annuity guaranty fund (or association) based on the Life and Health Insurance Guaranty Association Model Act adopted by NAIC. Like all model legislation, a NAIC model is subject to change as soon as the draft comes to the legislative floor. Variation has been greatly reduced in recent years as a result of NAIC's state certification program. To be certified, a state must adopt the NAIC-approved models without substantial change. NAIC certification has done much to increase uniformity between states, but there is still some variation.

HYPOTHETICAL INSOLVENCY

If we assume that the caller's company was insolvent, we get a clearer picture of how the system works. Let's assume that his imaginary company, Payless Annuity Insurance Company, was seized by the state insurance department and a court order has placed the company in rehabilitation and appointed the state insurance commissioner (or his deputy) as "receiver."

The receiver's first action is to place a moratorium on company payments except for necessary administrative expenses until the severity of the insolvency has been determined. In other words, the receiver will make no policy holder payments until the assets and liabilities are added up and the percentage that Payless can pay on each dollar is known.

While accountants are determining the payout percentage, the receiver notifies the National Association of Life and Health Guaranty Associations (N.O.L.H.G.A.). Instead of trying to deal with the association in each state where the company did business, the receiver works with the national organization, NOLHGA. Finally, a working document is presented to

NOLHGA. This "Assumption Document" lists[a]

- Each policy holder (sorted by state)
- Policy value
- Number of contracts
- Coinsurance
- Policy value less coinsurance
- State guaranty limit
- Amount not covered

This type of list is prepared for both annuity and/or life insurance policy holders.

Several important observations can be made from this example. First, the state of California has what is called a 20 percent "co-insurance" requirement. This is a 20 percent deductible *not* covered by the state guaranty fund. Fortunately for policy holders, this deductible is applied first, before the $100,000 state limit of coverage is applied.[b]

All Payless policies owned by the same individual are lumped together. It does not matter if a policy holder has one contract or ten. The $100,000 limit is applied to the *total*, not to individual contracts. The last column— the amount not covered—is the amount for which the annuitant may file a claim against the assets of Payless (along with all other creditors).

Usually the receiver cooperates with NOLHGA and solicits bids from other solvent insurance carriers to assume these contracts.[c] In most situations there is a separate assumption for life insurance and a separate assumption for annuity contracts. The assumption is for the *amount covered by guaranty funds*.

Fortunately, in many insolvencies the assuming company offers to take over the uncovered amount as well. The assuming company receives the

---

[a] See appendix I for an example of an Assumption Document based on an actual insurer insolvency.

[b] The deductible is more costly to administer than the savings it generates.

[c] Known as a reinsurance assumption.

payout percentage from the receiver. Additionally, a moratorium is placed on policy holder withdrawals for the time necessary for interest earnings to cover the shortage.

GUARANTY FUND LIMITS

When the questioner got word of Payless' insolvency, he may have rushed to get a copy of the state guarantee fund law. If he did, he read something like this:

> The contractual obligations of the insolvent insurer for which the association becomes or may become liable shall be in excess of $100 and shall be as great as but no greater than the contractual obligations of the insolvent insurer would have been in the absence of an insolvency.

A common feature of guarantee fund laws is a provision for a $100 deductible. In actual practice, NOLHGA (the national association of funds) usually convinces the state associations to dispense with the deductible.[3]

The jolting part of the law, at least for individuals with large life or annuity contracts, is the section dealing with the limit of coverage. That section usually reads

> But the aggregate liability of the association on any one life shall not exceed $100,000 with respect to the payment of cash values, or $300,000 for all benefits.

What is urgently important for policy holders is the phrase *"aggregate liability of the association on any one life."* Even if the policy is for one million dollars, the aggregate liability for the guarantee fund is $100,000—not $300,000. The $300,000 is for "all benefits."

It is understandable that someone reading the above could interpret it to mean that an annuitant or a life insurance policy holder would be paid up to $300,000. It is not uncommon to hear insurance professionals talking about $300,000 as the guaranty funds limit on a life contract. But the fact is,

NOLHGA and the individual state associations interpret the law to mean a *maximum of $100,000 per individual* (annuity or life insurance).

These organizations don't specify what other benefits might add up to $300,000. Whatever they may be, guaranty associations interpret the law to mean that for any one individual the limit is $100,000 for cash values. Therefore, no matter how large any one individual's policy/contract, payment from the guaranty association will be limited to cash values of $100,000. There will be no other payment for a life or annuity contract.

CONCLUSION

The information provided in this chapter is a very general look at the solvency issue. Much more could be written about insurance company solvency, and much more detail could be given about how an insolvency is administered.

Additionally, this information should not be viewed as critical of the guaranty fund system. It is a relatively new system and far better than the confusion that reigned before the model acts and before individual states passed guaranty funds legislation.

As with everything in life, change is certain. We should expect the insurance solvency and guarantee fund laws to change.

END NOTES

1. The first persons paid are new creditors: the bankruptcy administrators. In some states employees are paid before policyholders.

2. Policyholders are paid up to some limits before pre-existing *trade* creditors.

CHAPTER EIGHT

❖

FRAUD WATCH

When you write that check, what are you buying? The viatical industry has spawned a variety of schemes and fraud. Here's a sampling, and tips to help you avoid becoming a victim.

THE BIGGEST VIATICAL SCAM TO DATE—TOTALING $95 MILLION AND affecting investors nationwide—made headlines in April 1997. Sixteen hundred people had invested as much as $300,000 each, based on promises of annual interest payments of 25 percent.[1] The U.S. attorney's office charged three men and a woman with fraud.

Personal Choice Opportunities (PCO) based in Palm Springs, California, was charged with inducing investors to "lend" funds to PCO to finance viatical settlements. Investors came from 24 states and included brokers who put in their own money along with their clients's funds.

This was nothing more than a Ponzi scheme.[a] None of the funds were used to purchase a single life insurance policy.[2] PCO fabricated patients, insurance policies, and medical records. Life expectancy estimates for these non-existent patients were provided by Thomas K. Hines, M.D., of Valley Medical Center, Carson City, Nevada. A Las Vegas, Nevada attorney, John Tom Ross, provided his legal opinion that viatical investments were not securities.[b]

Some of the funds from new investors were used to pay previous investors, but not all.

> David Laing [the principal] used more than $30 million of investors' money for personal expenses, including $10 million gambling in Las Vegas.[3]

On the surface, PCO seemed to be a typical viatical company. PCO even used an escrow trust to hold investor money. This was not a bank escrow account, however. Escrow Plus of Burbank, California, was involved in the deception. Escrow Plus is alleged "to have stonewalled regulators's efforts to obtain copies of the policies by claiming patient confidentiality." [4]

It's interesting to note how the victims found PCO. One of PCO's principals appeared on numerous radio programs. He also used the Internet to attract investors, through Web sites set up with different company names and through posts sent to various investment news groups.

Some investors heard about this company from an insurance broker. At least one California investor was drawn in by a broker. Fifty investors from

---

[a] Initially, all defendants were released on bail, and PCO and Escrow Plus continued to be open for business. Seven months after the initial charge David Laing admitted to the fraud and his attorney, Robert. L. Shapiro (of O.J. Simpson renown) admitted it was a Ponzi scheme. See end notes 2 and 5.

[b] Information about the doctor and lawyer provided by Melinda Brun, Esq., senior trial counsel, California Department of Corporations, who is prosecuting the case.

Montana put nearly $2.2 million into the company.[5] Thirty-one of these investors were clients of an investment advisor for First Securities USA. They invested $1.44 million. Seventeen others, clients of another First Securities USA investment advisor, put up more than $600,000. Others investors were individual clients of two insurance agents who were not licensed to sell securities. They were persuaded to part with $100,000 and $40,000, respectively.[6]

MUTUAL BENEFITS

Two Florida men who controlled Florida-based Mutual Benefits Corporation (MBC), were charged with fraud by the Securities and Exchange Commission. Without admitting or denying the allegations the principals of MBC, considered to be of the nation's largest viatical companies, agreed to settle the charges brought by the SEC.

Joel Steinger and his brother Leslie Steinger were charged with

> selling unregistered securities in violation of Section 5of the Securities Actof 1933 (Securities Act), andwith misrepresentation in violation of Section 17(a) of the Securities Act and Section 10(b) of the Securities Exchange Act of 1934, and Rule 10b-5 thereunder.[7]

They are alleged to have misled 1,190 investors in connection with the sale of $100 million worth of unregistered viatical settlements. Investors were told

> they held irrevocable interests in these life insurance policies when they did not. They were told their funds were held in a "Special Trust Account" when the account was nothing more than an MBC checking account.
> The Steingers also misled investors by failing to disclose that investor funds would typically be held by MBC for several weeks or more prior to being placed on a policy, thereby negatively affecting the investment's annual rate of return.

This was the first, albeit small success for the SEC in its efforts to regulate the viatical investment industry.[8]

DIGNITY PARTNERS

Dignity Partners was a leading viatical company, large, well-financed, and respected. It no longer exists except on court documents filed in federal court where it stands accused of fraud.

Dignity was the first viatical funding firm listed on the stock market. A month after the company went public in March 1996, the Vancouver AIDS Conference was held. From this conference the world learned about trial runs of a new 3-drug combination that included a new drug: protease inhibitors. The experimental drugs were capable of wiping out detectable levels of the HIV virus in AIDS patients. This was the first AIDS therapy that had potential to lengthen the life span as well as improve the health of many terminally ill patients.

The news devastated Dignity Partners. AIDS patients comprised 95 percent of the company's insurance portfolio—valued at $56 million at "maturity." Almost overnight Dignity's stock price dropped 31 percent. By July, their stock was down 77 percent.

Dignity's first reaction was to suspend further purchases until it examined the implications of the Vancouver conference. Within a year the company was a memory—or a nightmare, if you were one of thousands of investors who bought Dignity stock at $12 and $14 dollars a share.

There are lessons to be learned from the saga of Dignity Partners. One lesson is that securities laws don't offer as much protection as we may wish. In December 1996, three shareholders filed a class action lawsuit in federal court in California. They charged the company and its individual directors with violations of federal securities laws.[a]

The lead plaintiffs who collectively lost nearly $300,000, allege that Dignity and its directors filed false and misleading financial statements with the Securities Exchange Commission. These financial statements, they claim,

---

[a] Case #C-96-4558-CAL, filed in United States District Court, Northern District of California, December 16, 1996.

inflated the company's revenue, assets, and net worth. They also allege that mischievous accounting procedures allowed Dignity to hide the fact it was undercapitalized. Dignity vehemently denies each allegation.

Most significant for potential investors is the charge that Dignity paid unrealistically high prices for policies: [9]

> Dignity did not utilize known adverse information (including . . . historical data reflecting the true value of its insurance portfolio and the accuracy of its life estimates) . . . [a]

Dignity admits they ignored medical consultants' advice because o f competition for policies.[b] This is a highly credible argument since viatical firms to this day complain of too few policies in the marketplace and that unlicensed companies drive up prices in order to corner the market.

The suit also accuses Dignity of faulty medical underwriting. Dignity is alleged to have had knowledge of protease inhibitors long before the Vancouver Conference—and months before the stock offering. As evidence, the plaintiffs point to one of Dignity's board members, Dr. Paul A. Volberding, a highly esteemed physician with considerable experience in AIDS research and treatment.

Thus, Dignity is accused of not utilizing information about protease inhibitors, with the result that

> A significant number of the policies insuring people with AIDS were not collectible within the time period established . . . . [c]

In other words, a large number of policies did not "mature" within the assigned life expectancy. Dignity refutes this, claiming there is no evidence that

---

[a] Page 22 of the class action lawsuit.

[b] The company admitted to this in its 10-Q filing with the SEC.

[c] Page 17 of the class action lawsuit.

viators whose policies they owned were taking the new "3-drug cocktail."

Dignity also claims that no evidence was presented to show that Dr. Volberding "participated in the day-to-day corporate activities" or communicated information to the corporation about experimental medical drugs.[10] In fact, Dignity states that while 18 percent of polices were overdue, 20 percent were collectible earlier than their estimated maturity dates.

Whether these shareholders are poor sports—people who took a risk, lost, and cried "Foul!"—or whether their claims rest on bedrock will be decided when evidence is presented at court. It may turn out that Dignity is innocent of all charges, but Dignity was never the shining star most people believed. On at least four occasions Dignity Partners violated California's viatical regulations.

The first known incident occurred when a viator, Brian,[a] asked the author to review documents he was about to sign to transfer ownership of his policy to Dignity Partners. Brian saw nothing amiss, since he was unfamiliar with California viatical law. His anxiety was due to a pound of unfamiliar legal documents. As it turned out, he had cause to be concerned.

What Brian didn't know was that licensed companies are required by law to establish an escrow trust at "a qualified, licensed financial institution." One page in his transfer packet revealed that Dignity's escrow account was a private trust in the name of one of the principals of Dignity Partners. This same principal served as trustee.

In view of Dignity's reputation, this was more than odd. Applicants for viatical licenses must supply the Department of Insurance with a list of

financial institutions(s) and/or resource(s) where future viaticum is maintained.

They also must submit copies of these escrow agreements. Since Dignity Partners was a licensed viatical funding firm, it must have complied with these

---

[a] A fictitious name. As in "Cash for the Final Days," viators' true identities are not disclosed.

requirements when they applied for a license. At some later time a switch was made. When? Why? We may never know.

Brian made a copy of the document, which the author forwarded to Nancy Ayoob, a staff attorney at the California Department of Insurance. At that time Ms. Ayoob was responsible for overseeing compliance with viatical regulations. Shortly thereafter, Ms. Ayoob reported that Dignity Partners had agreed to reinstate the proper escrow trust.

The second violation is well known, since Dignity announced it to the press. In 1995, they repackaged $35 million worth of life insurance, which they sold to a Connecticut-based investment bank. The policies had been purchased from 300 viators, mainly AIDS patients, none with life expectancies greater than three years. Before marketing the policies, Dignity had them rated by Standard & Poor's. They were assigned an "A" rating.[11]

This sale was illegal.[12] California's viatical regulations, along with regulations from the states of Washington, Illinois, and a few others, prohibit licensed companies from reselling policies to any but another viatical company licensed by the state insurance department.[a]

This prohibition is for the protection of viators. If a licensed company resells a policy to an unlicensed one, viators' medical confidentiality may be breached by illegal companies who use their medical records as marketing tools. Viators' privacy rights may also be breached since illegal companies often harass viators with frequent telephone calls.

Dignity's third violation was prompted by its haste to liquidate assets. It sold most of its portfolio to Mutual Benefits Corporation, a Florida-based viatical company with a long history of opposition to viatical regulation.[13] One problem with this sale was that Mutual Benefits was not licensed in

---

[a] California's regulations are not as explicit as those of Washington State. Since it's an interpretation of existing provisions rather than an actual statute, if viatical companies are held accountable, they may challenge the interpretation in court.

California.[a] Another, that the principals of Mutual Benefits were known to be unprincipled, at best.

Dignity's liquidation of policies through sale to Mutual Benefits was a loss of $3 million to the company and shareholders.[b] Despite the loss, it wasn't long before the partners regrouped as Point West Capital and made plans to re-enter the viatical business.

The collapse of Dignity came as a shock to all who were familiar with the viatical industry. Dignity treated viators well and paid fairly and on time. One has to wonder how those viators are faring now, as assets of the redoubtable Mutual Benefits.[14]

Dignity did not sell everything. They had no choice but to keep at least one policy—the one for which a lawsuit was pending. When this case was fought in the courts of Massachusetts, Dignity's reputation suffered another blow. This incident, more than any other, had consequences for the entire viatical industry, the insurance industry, all investors, and anyone who, in future years, buys life insurance to protect their loved ones. The story follows.

VIATORS AND FRAUD

Dennis J. Sullivan was diagnosed with HIV in November 1990, at which time he "began a course of treatment including use of the drug AZT."[15] Ten months later, in September 1991, Sullivan applied to Protective Life for a life insurance policy with a death benefit of $100,000. This had to be term insurance, since the annual premium was minuscule: $175, which included the cost for the disability waiver of premium.

> In his application, Sullivan falsely stated that he was not taking any medication, and he omitted the names of those doctors who knew of his diagnosis.

---

[a] Mutual Benefits was not licensed anywhere until late 1997, when it acquired a license in Florida. See end notes for more details.

[b] Documented in Dignity's SEC filings and on page 17 of the class action lawsuit.

The insurer, Protective Life, issued the policy without ordering an HIV or other medical test. By June 1992, when Sullivan's HIV had progressed to AIDS, he stopped working. Sullivan could have applied for the premium waiver, but he continued paying the premium until November. Then, exactly two years after Protective Life issued the policy, Sullivan filed a claim for the disability waiver.

In the fall of 1993, Sullivan enlisted the aid of a viatical broker to sell his policy.[a] The broker contacted Protective Life for information about Sullivan's life insurance, then arranged for the sale of the policy to Dignity Partners for $73,000.

Dignity Partners delivered the assignment forms to Protective Life on December 14, 1993. The transfer was approved by the insurer on December 22, 1993, and Dignity paid Sullivan that same day.

Sullivan died in 1995, and Dignity Partners collected the full death benefit of $100,000. But Protective was not happy about paying this claim. It "sued in federal court to recover the money, alleging Dignity knew of Sullivan's fraud."

A federal judge ruled in Protective's favor and Dignity appealed, thus pouring more dollars into legal fees. This time Dignity was victorious.[b]

The Supreme Judicial Council of Massachusetts ruled unanimously that the Massachusetts incontestability statute barred life insurers from voiding a policy after the two-year window closes—even if an insurer eventually discovers fraud.

Did Dignity Partners have knowledge about the viator's fraud? Clues were there—sprinkled throughout two years' worth of medical records.

---

[a] The role of viatical brokers is described in chapter 3, "Cash for the Final Days."

[b] This victory was great news for Dignity, but look at the cost: federal court, then the appeals court, and huge legal fees, totalling perhaps more than the profit from this policy.

IMPOSTERS

Another insurer, faced with a similar case of fraud, didn't bother taking the matter to court. It simply refused to pay the death benefits. This case involved another California-based viatical firm.

This insurer, Amex Life Assurance, required a blood test and medical examination. In 1991, Jose Morales applied for a $180,000 life insurance policy. Two years earlier he had tested positive for HIV. Nevertheless, when he applied for insurance Morales failed to disclose his HIV status. Then he sent an imposter to take the medical examination in his place.

Two years and one month after the policy was issued Morales died of AIDS-related causes. By that time, the policy had been sold to a licensed viatical firm, Los Angeles-based Access Program, also known as Slome Capital Corporation.[a]

An anonymous phone call tipped off Amex Life to the imposter. The height and weight of the two men were different, and the imposter was a smoker, which the insured was not. When the insurer refused to pay the death claim, Access Program sued for "breach of contract," "insurance bad faith," and "equitable estoppable." [16]

The case began in superior court in Los Angeles, California, and concluded at the court of appeal. Despite a finding that Mr. Morales engaged in "gross and willful fraud with the intent of deceiving Amex," the court upheld the incontestability clause. Access was paid.[b]

Although some courts have decided imposter cases in favor of insurers,[c]

---

[a] Access Program's brochure, distributed to AIDS organizations, announced that it was a licensed company when its license was only pending approval. The author turned this evidence over to the Department of Insurance.

[b] The costs of the legal battle may have contributed to the demise of Access. The company no longer exists.

[c] In some states, if an imposter takes the medical exam or gives blood for the applicant, insurance companies may consider the imposter to be the insured. In such a case, they have

the California court decided that "a cheat who signs the false application and who thereafter sends the imposter to the medical examination successfully cheats the insurer after two years."[17]

The California court suggested that insurers might avoid imposter problems if they required "photographic identification before conducting a medical exam and issuing a policy."[18] Aside from this advice, the Court did not comment on the burden its ruling placed on insurers or on viatical companies. To better understand what this ruling means for viatical companies and investors, see chapter 9, "Viators and Fraud."

In recent years there has been a rash of fraud cases. In most, though not all, the insured died of AIDS. Industry watchers foresee increases in these cases, due to home-based anonymous HIV tests and to drug therapies that appear to wipe out all traces of HIV.[19]

In nearly every case that reached court, the incontestability clause barred insurers from canceling policies based on fraud. And while judges are fond of noting that they don't condone fraud, they have yet to comment on the conduct of viatical companies that buy such policies, supposedly on the basis of close scrutiny of medical records in which symptoms and treatments are noted and a diagnosis made prior to the insurance application.

Naturally, the viatical companies deny any such knowledge. They would have us think they didn't draw any conclusions from their perusal of viator records.

This disclaimer is challenged by Robert Shear, president of the Viatical Association of America and principal at a leading viatical funding firm:

> If a company buys a policy, knowing the viator was diagnosed before applying and lied on the application, and the company collaborates in the fraud . . . is that morally okay? And is the investor who buys this policy a party to the fraud? [20]

Although the incontestability clause protects investors most of the time,

---

no obligation to pay upon the death of the person who signed the application.

investors shouldn't bet their savings on it—as the following case shows.

WHEN FRAUD LOSES

This case has many twists, including implications of collaboration with insurance agents. It began when Anthony Fioretti applied to Columbian Mutual in January 1987 for a $100,000 policy. A blood test required by the insurer revealed that Fioretti was HIV positive, and the application was rejected.

The following month Fioretti applied to Massachusetts General, this time for a death benefit just shy of $2 million. On his application Anthony C. Fioretti represented his name as "C. Tony Fioretti." His actual date of birth, September 6, 1948, was represented as "3-6-47." The Social Security number was not the same as the one listed with Columbian Mutual. And, Fioretti stated that he had never been denied insurance, nor consulted any physicians, and that he had no known health conditions. [21]

This time, when Fioretti was required to take a blood test for HIV, he arranged for an imposter to be tested under his name. The policy was issued.

In December of that year Fioretti applied to add the premium waiver to his policy. It was more than six months since the first blood test, and he was required to undergo a second HIV test. Once more, an imposter substituted for Fioretti.

> On the strength of this test result and Anthony Fioretti's execution of a second Statement of Good Health, MassGen approved Anthony Fioretti's Waiver of Premium. [22]

On February 28, 1989, just past the second anniversary of the policy, Fioretti, now a resident of Florida, died of AIDS. In April his brother Vincent filed a beneficiary claim. In December, MassGen denied the claim and refunded the premiums paid under the policy. Vincent Fioretti rejected these premiums, and MassGen filed an action in Superior Court of New Jersey, seeking recession (cancellation) of the policy. [a]

This action was dismissed by the court for lack of personal jurisdiction over the beneficiary, who was a resident of Florida. Vincent Fioretti then turned to the circuit court in Florida. MassGen filed a counterclaim, seeking recession, and had the case removed to district court. Now it was July 1990—more than a year had passed since the insured's demise.

MassGen argued that an "imposter defense" removes the bar on coverage disputes otherwise imposed by the incontestability clause. The district court agreed, and Fioretti appealed.

Now the federal court had to decide on the "imposter defense." They looked to the laws of New Jersey, where the last act necessary to complete the insurance contract was performed. The court found a recent New Jersey supreme court decision that "explicitly stated that this [contestability] statute does not prevent an insurer from denying coverage when its insured has committed fraud in securing coverage."

New Jersey has a volume of court cases in which fraud supercedes the incontestability clause. But a 1990 case best explains the rationale of that state's courts. The case involved William Penn Life Insurance and a $140,000 life insurance policy issued on the life of Steven Ledley.

One month after the policy was issued, the insured died of heart failure. Since this was within the contestability period, William Penn conducted a vigorous investigation. They learned that Ledley had failed to disclose an extensive history of thyroid problems, as well as the possibility of cancer which was revealed through tests taken for the thyroid problems.

On the application Ledley stated that he had not consulted other physicians, "when he had, in fact, consulted two other physicians" as well as the treating physician. [23]

The appeals court upheld New Jersey's lower court: The insured's false

---

[a] If Fioretti had accepted the premium refund, the result would have been the same as if the policy had never existed.

statements were declared to be fraud. Since the insurer relied on these "material misrepresentations" when it issued the policy, and since this caused the insurer to be defrauded, William Penn was allowed to void the contract.

FRAUD AND OTHER STATES

Massachusetts and California are among the states whose laws deny insurers the right to void a policy on the basis of fraud. But there are a number of states where fraud supersedes the incontestability clause.[24] And on the federal level, fraud supersedes the incontestability clause in regard to Federal Employees Government Life Insurance (FEGLI) policies.

What this means to investors is that you can't be certain if you're buying something that is worthless unless you're certain that the policy was not issued on the basis of fraud. It *is* possible to avoid these risks, as attorney David Wood explains in Chapter 9.[25]

If you're wondering about the ability of terminally ill patients to plan and execute such a scheme, remember that they have done so for hundreds of years. This has been a continuing problem for insurers. The big difference nowadays is that patients are assisted by unscrupulous insurance agents.

These life insurance agents have helped some patients paint a new face on fraud. The agents seek insurers whose death benefit limits don't require a blood test. In some cases agents encourage insureds to apply for multiple policies with different insurers, each policy within these non-medical limits.[a] Then the patients sell the bundle of policies—during the contestability period.

Investors are tempted to buy these policies with claims of returns of 100 percent or higher.[b] Such returns may be possible since, due to the great risk, these policies are sold at 10 or 15 percent of the death benefit.

Some people might think it clever for terminally ill people to acquire

---

[a] If death benefits are within nonmedical limits, no medical tests are required—unless an applicant admits to an adverse health condition.

[b] See Conclusion, for a sample of how this is sold.

bundles of policies and sell them at 10 or 15 percent of face value. Stealing from insurance companies might seem like a small crime or a deserved penalty for insurers, who are generally detested by the public. But consider the result. The rest of us, when we want to buy life insurance, will pay the tab through higher premiums.

Meanwhile, this type of fraud holds the possibility of turning some viators into overnight millionaires. This is no exaggeration. One agent advertised in a newspaper: "If you are HIV positive, I can make you a millionaire."

In the Ledley case cited above, beneficiaries tried to transfer blame to the agent who took the application. In that case the court found no facts to support fault on the part of the agent. Next time, they might find fault.

James E. Melville, president of Universal Guaranty Life Insurance Company of Springfield, Illinois, discovered agents within his company who were actively soliciting prospective insureds with health conditions. These agents had already placed policies totaling $23 million in death benefits. More policies totaling $17 million, written by the same agents, were in the process of being underwritten when Melville exposed the scheme.[26]

Melville told another story: A policyholder had been insured for $250,000 for 15 years. He went to a viatical company to sell his policy. The company's agents proposed a deal. If the insured would sell the policy at a bargain price, they would get him a replacement policy with a $100,000 face amount. He agreed, and they did as promised.

In another situation a Miami insurance agent distributed brochures that stated,

If you are HIV positive. . . You probably think you can't purchase life insurance. Now you can!

The award-winning agent who sponsored these brochures is Phillip Scott Plotka, a Certified Life Underwriter (CLU) who served on a professional advisory committee for the insurance industry. Plotka was contacted by a man who claimed to be recently diagnosed as HIV-positive, who wanted life insurance but had misgivings about disclosing his medical condition to an insurance company. Plotka assisted the man in his application for $50,000 in life insurance coverage, and advised the client to lie in response to medical questions related to the diagnosis. The client was an undercover state insurance fraud investigator.[27]

In May 1998 Florida officials arrested John L. Cote, 53, and charged him with false and fraudulent insurance application. Cote had tried to sell a $95,000 life insurance policy which was acquired by denying on the application that he had been diagnosed with AIDS. In this situation, a viatical company alerted the insurer to the fraud when Cote tried to viaticate his policy.[28]

These stories strengthen Melville's point about the potential for fraud in viatical settlements. But Melville didn't name the viatical company that made the deal. We don't know if this company was licensed or if it operated illegally. Care should be taken not to lump together illegal companies with legal ones. Although Melville would prefer to "do away with viaticals," that is tantamount to throwing out the baby with the bath water.

Instead, steps could be taken to protect insurers and, ultimately, future policy holders:

♦ All states should require licensing of companies that buy policies from terminally ill insureds.

♦ Insurers should closely examine business as it comes in. As Melville says,

If an agent starts writing a disproportionate amount of out-of-state policies near the blood limits, watch out.

In addition, the National Association of Insurance Commissioners (NAIC) should urge state legislatures to modify incontestability statutes to allow rescission of life insurance policies when there is evidence of intentional fraud within three or four years of the date a policy was issued.[a]

---

[a] Texas has court rulings that establish this precedent. The key concept is "intentional" fraud.

MULTINATIONAL LIFE INSURANCE

Although viatical settlements have existed for years in Europe, it's the rare European who is aware of this. These are private transactions. Europe doesn't have a formal industry. Thus, would-be viators are eager to sell their policies to investors in the U.S.[a] And U.S.-based viatical companies are eager to get these policies since there are too few to meet the demand of this flourishing industry. One question investors should ask is, "Why would Europeans or Australians, or Canadians want to sell their policies to Americans?"

Clearly, the market that exists in the U.S. doesn't exist in European countries. Additionally, these viators have more privacy by selling to U.S.-based companies. Not only is tracking more difficult but also more expensive when the viator is a continent away. It's a situation that could lead to large-scale fraud.

Another reason may be that Europeans can get larger viaticums from Americans. This is especially true if the company that arranges the sale doesn't invest for itself but earns fees as a go-between. Since fees charged by these companies are related to purchase price, not death benefits, the higher purchase price yields higher commissions for salespeople.

Third, illegal U.S.-based companies can more readily transact business with international viators and investors than with companies that abide by the laws. As an added plus, international buyers and sellers usually are unaware that these companies are violating local or national law.

Life Partners, which vowed never to be licensed, boasts of doing business in Europe. It's likely that other illegal companies do this, as well.

A few licensed companies have moved beyond U.S. borders. One U.S.-licensed company with a presence in Canada is Michigan-based Accelerated Benefits Capital, which has an affiliate office in Montreal. Another viatical company is associated with C.N.A., the parent company of Viaticus. Both of these companies seek Canadian viators; neither sells policies to the public. But

---

[a] The single Canadian company is Montreal-based Life Source & Associates/Source de vie.

numerous illegal companies operate in Canada, as well— including some in Ontario, where such sales are prohibited.

The Ontario Securities Commission (OSCB) is aware that viatical investments are marketed in Ontario and that "registrants are being approached as potential sales agents." As a result, the OSCB published a notice warning investors and sales agents that viatical sales are considered securities.[29]

Under Ontario's Security Act the purchase by a single investor who becomes sole owner of a policy would be considered a security if, for example,

> the investor relies on the intermediary to select and evaluate the policy(ies), to monitor the health of the insured and to collect the benefits.

So, too, if co-owners buy fractionalized shares:

> If the viatical settlement takes the form of a fractional interest in a pool of benefit payments, the settlement is simply an asset-backed security, and as such is a security for purposes of the Act.

If you're offered an investment in a policy that insures a patient in another country, be aware that these sales may be illegal. If the sale violates local law—whether it's state, regional, or national law, the contract could be voided by local authorities. If that happens, your investment is worthless.

HOW TO PROTECT YOURSELF FROM FRAUD

The following advice is an amalgam created from various government publications and adapted specifically to viatical investments:

- ◆ Don't expect to get rich quick. Your chances of doing so are about equal to those of winning the lottery jackpot.
- ◆ Be wary of references to investors who made fortunes. These people could be in on the scam, or they may be innocent investors whose

payoff was part of a pyramid scheme.[a]

♦ Remember: the greater the potential reward, the greater the potential risk. This is always true no matter what promoters tell you.

♦ Be especially wary when someone tells you profits will be great enough to offset the risk.

♦ Don't assume that online computer service police the investment bulletin boards. Most don't.

♦ Don't act on the advice of a person who appears to be wealthy and successful or who uses church or club membership to gain your trust.

♦ "Avoid any investment touted as `IRS Approved' or otherwise endorsed by the IRS. This is a *clear* sign of trouble . . . The IRS does *not* endorse specific tax deals." [30]

♦ Do your own research. Investigate. Get all the information you can. If none is available, don't sign that check.

HOW TO SPOT A CON ARTIST

Who would imagine meeting a con artist at church or temple? Especially if that someone has elegant clothes, a corporate jet, luxury vehicles, and travels internationally. Who wouldn't be impressed when he boasts of "making huge profits buying and selling Eurobonds and trading commodities on the Chicago Mercantile Exchange"? [31]

This glamorous salesman really exists. His name is Harry J. Sherbody. In 1994, at the age of 42, Harry Sherbody was sentenced to more than eight years in federal prison for a multimillion dollar Ponzi scheme that cost some investors their life savings. But Sherbody is not the only swindler in sheep's clothing.

> There are case histories in which individuals who held positions of trust and esteem—accountants, attorneys, bona fide investment brokers and even doctors—have sacrificed

---

[a] Pyramid schemes pay the early investors with monies taken from later investors.

their ethics for the fast buck of running an investment scam.[32]

In one such case a Los Angeles grandmother, Joan Pierre, lost her home to a "Bible-toting huckster" who swindled her out of $16,000. It began when Pierre had financial difficulties and Barnett, the huckster, who was out on bail, brought her a proposition. He would lower her monthly mortgage payments from $1,689 to $461. Barnett pocketed the $461 a month that Pierre paid him, but the mortgage didn't get paid. The bank foreclosed on Pierre's house, evicting the grandmother, her grandchildren, and an elderly aunt.[33]

> They may wear three-piece suits or they may wear hard hats. They may have no apparent connection to the investment business or they may have an alphabet-soup of impressive letters following their names. They may be glib and fast-talking or so seemingly shy and soft-spoken that you feel almost compelled to force your money on them.[34]

HOW TO LISTEN TO A CON ARTIST

Listen with two sets of ears—your own and those of a companion. Don't meet with a sales person alone. Tape record the discussion. Then you can review it later to find out if questions were answered or ignored, and if answers match what is in the brochure and contract.

Remember, whether someone is honest won't be revealed by their dress, car, lifestyle, educational achievements, profession, or age. Far too often seniors are duped by kindly folk in their sixties and older.

Those who are inclined to give automatic trust to attorneys should know that lawyers' theft of clients' assets led the California State Bar to set up a fund to reimburse clients victimized by their attorneys.

> Swindlers attempt to mimic the sales approaches of legitimate investment firms and salespersons.[35]

Remember Personal Choice Opportunities (PCO), mentioned at the start of this chapter? Remember their affiliate, Escrow Plus? These swindlers succeeded in mimicking legitimate viatical companies, to the tune of $95 million garnered from investors in many states.

It may be easy to discredit sales promoters who claim there is no risk. But there are sales promoters who

> to make themselves more credible, acknowledge some risk—then quickly reassure you it's minimal in relation to the profits you will almost certainly make. [36]

A clear example of this is the slogan you'll hear from those who promote policies that are contestable:

> Minimal risk in relation to profits.

The greatest risks result when investors fall victim to one of the various faces of fraud. In chapter 9 attorney David Wood explains how viatical companies can take steps to avoid viator fraud.

END NOTES

1. Debora Vrana, "U.S. Charges Four with Fraud in Life Insurance Investment Case." *Los Angeles Times,* April 22, 1997.

2. "California Man Admits to Viatical Fraud." *Los Angeles Times,* November 14, 1997. David Laing, 53, pleaded guilty to cheating 1,600 investors out of $95 million in a scheme involving false purchases of insurance policies from the terminally ill. Laing and his co-conspirators pocketed the money or used it to cover expenses.

3. *The Billings Gazette.*

4. Gail Diane Cox, "Growth Market in Death Futures Spawns Suits." *National Law Journal,*"The New York Law Publishing Co., May 26, 1997. Available: http://ljx.com/practice/intellectualpro...3097/rotation./topstories/0523new2. html

5. "State Sues Seven Defendants for Investment Fraud," Marilyn Scanlon, Bureau Chief, Idaho Securities Bureau, April 11, 1997.

6. Joe Kolman, "Montanans Lose Money in $95 Million Scam." *The Billings Gazette,* May 20, 1998. In Montana, as in many other states, fractionalized shares are considered securities and must be registered with the state securities department.

7. SEC v. Joel Steinger and Leslie Steinger, *SEC News Digest,* May 4, 1998. Available: gov.us.fed.sec.announce.
  The Steingers agreed to an entry of a judgment permanently enjoining them from violating the registration and antifraud provisions of the federal securities laws, and payment of a total of $850,000 in disgorgement and interest, and to pay $50,000 each in civil money penalties.

8. The SEC believes viatical investments should be regulated as securities. Leo Orenstein, the lead attorney in the SEC's case against Life Partners, filed for another court hearing in April 1997. On November 26, 1997, Judge Royce C. Lamberth ordered a summary judgment against the SEC for failing to present material evidence to support its position. Now it appears that the SEC will continue its efforts to regulate this industry one step at a time, beginning with Mutual Benefits. [Summary of court decision provided by R. Scott Peden, General Counsel for Life Partners, Inc.]

END NOTES

9. *Howard Hertzberg, et al., On Behalf of Themselves and All Others Similarly Situated v. Dignity Partners, Inc., et al,* United States District Court Northern District of California, No, C-96-4558-CAL. Available: http://securities.stanford.edu/briefs/dignity/96cv04558/025.html.

10. Defendant's Motion to Dismiss, June 20, 1997.

11. Arthur M. Louis, "S.F. Investment Company Sells `Death Notes.'" *San Francisco Chronicle*, March 4, 1995.

12. Attorney Caitlin Smith of California's department of insurance (DOI) explained DOI's position in regard to resale of a viator's policy to an unlicensed entity. It is illegal under § 1013.2 of the Insurance Code, as "contrary to the public interest." The DOI had the ability to enforce this, Ms. Smith said, and would go after violators with a choice of remedies:

♦ The DOI could revoke the license of violators
♦ The DOI could void the sale under subsection "c," which requires all forms used by the viatical company to be approved by the DOI
♦ The DOI could void the sale under subsection "m," (false or misleading solicitations), since viators were led to believe they were selling to a company that was regulated, which meant their rights were protected;
♦ The DOI could void the sale under contract law. The second purchaser, who is unlicensed, is stepping into the place of the first buyer.

Note: The above information was provided by attorney Caitlin Smith in a telephone conversation with the author, September 9, 1997. However, it was neither confirmed nor denied by the press release department of the DOI, which chose to take no public position on this matter. It's a gray area of existing law, and may not be accepted if challenged in court by a viatical company. Until then, viatical companies should consider this to be a warning.

13. Mutual Benefits buys from viators and resells to investors. Its investor packet touts viaticals as

a fully secured, non-speculative financial opportunity.

Investors are told they can expect security and stability, an unequaled principal to profit ratio and

END NOTES

> a dramatic return on your money while eliminating the risks inherent in other high yielding instruments.

The brochure emphasized the killing power of AIDS, downplayed the ability of AZT, DDC and other medical regimens to extend a patient's life by more than a few months, and assured that, by submitting a patient's records to review by independent physicians as well as the patient's own doctor, Mutual Benefits could achieve

> a high degree of accuracy' in predicting an ill person's life span.

Source: Arthur Allen, "As They Lay Dying." *Washington Post,* November 17, 1997.

14. According to Arthur Allen Mutual Benefits is one of the big buyers of Medical Escrow's policies. Medical Escrow of Tavares, Florida, offers to buy policies from "anyone with T-cell counts up to 1,000." As author Allen says, "Normally, 1,000 is the T-cell count of a healthy person." Medical Escrow's explanation is that the viator may be HIV-positive but doesn't have full-blown AIDS yet. The offer may be no more than 30 percent "but we'll find a buyer."

15. *Ibid.*

16. Mark F. Hughes, Jr, ."Insurer's Ability to Contest Claims after the Contestability Cutoff." *Defense Counsel Journal,* October 1996.

17. George B. Kozol, "Home HIV Tests Create New Problems: Some May Fraudulently Purchase Life Insurance to Fund Medical Care." *Best's Review,* Life-Health Insurance Edition, December 1996.

18. In order to deter the use of imposters for medical exams, Senate Bill 1706, proposed in 1998, "would void a life insurance policy if an imposter is substituted during enrollment process, contingent on the insurer having made a photo identification of the applicant."

19. Shear's viatical funding firm, Accelerated Benefits Capital (Michigan and Montreal) buys for its own portfolio and has no plans to offer investments to individuals.

20. *Fioretti v. Massachusetts General Life Insurance Co.,* United States Court of Appeals, Eleventh Circuit, No. 93-5187, appealed from the U.S. District Court for the Southern District of Florida. (No. 90-06530-CIV-SM)
Available: http://www.law.emory.edu/1circuit/june95/93-5187.opa.html.

END NOTES

21. *Ibid.*

22. *Janice Ledley v. William Penn Life Insurance Co., et al.* No. A-35, Supreme Court of New Jersey, September term, 1994.

17. Quoted from Jack R. Nelson and Patricia J. Austin, "... And Materiality Restricts the Right to Rescind." *The National Law Journal,* September 8, 1997. "Under New York law, for example, the insurer has an absolute right to rescind a life insurance policy if the application, signed by the insured and attached to the policy, contains false statements or omissions about medical history. False statements or omissions about health are conclusively presumed to be material."

19. Some states consider a life insurance policy incontestable after two years except for nonpayment of premiums, prohibited risks, or additional insurance benefits such as disability payments or accidental death. Several states (e.g., Indiana insurance code 27-1-12-6 and Ohio insurance code 3915.05) include the following:

> That all statements made by the insured in the application shall, in the absence of fraud, be deemed representations and not warranties.

These phrases could be interpreted to allow a court to void a contract issued on the basis of fraud. And it does raise the hackles of some judges when they are faced with a victim of fraud who seems to have no legal remedies. The Kansas court of appeals, for example, took umbrage when a doctor's fraudulent acts prevented a patient from discovering the doctor's malpractice for so many years that the suffering patient no longer had the right to sue (because of the statute of limitations). The court ruled that the patient did have recourse, other than malpractice. She could sue for fraud.

> The statute of limitations in an action for relief on the ground of fraud does not start to run until the plaintiff discovers the fraud or until the plaintiff learns such facts as would lead a reasonably prudent person to investigate.

Deanna Robinson v. Nasreen B. Shah, M.D., No. 75,665, April 18, 1997. This case implies that an insurer who has no remedies at law to cancel a contract based on fraud (i.e., "material misrepresentation") may choose, instead, to sue for fraud.

END NOTES

26. Charles E. Schmidt, Jr., "Shady Agent, Viatical Mix Creates Recipe for Fraud," *Best's Review*, Life-Health Insurance Edition, March 1996. This article summarizes Melville's report to the National Alliance of Life Companies' fall 1995 meeting. Available. http://www.northernlight.com/cgi-bin/pdse...7020071841&ho=typhoon&po=5004&pc=-1#start.

27. Plotka was arrested on charges of grand theft, communications fraud, fraudulent insurance claims, and filing a false isnruance application. The penalty for these charges could be up to 30 years in the Florida State Prison system. Source: Florida Department of Insurance Press Release, and America Online news service, May 7, 1998.

28. "Man Charged with Fraud." *Sun-Sentinel*, May 16, 1998.

29. *Ontario Securities Commission Notices*, #44-Viatical Settlements, 19 O.S.C.B. 4680, 8/30/1996.

30.
"Bogus `IRS Approved' Investment Schemes." Published by the North America Securities Administrators Association (NASAA). Available:http://www.nasaa.org/investoredu/investoralerts/bogusira.html

31. Susan Gembrowski, "Businessman Gets Prison Term for Fraud," *San Diego Transcript*, December 6, 1994.

32. "Investment Swindles: How They Work and How to Avoid Them." Published by National Futures Association. Available: gopher://gopher.gsa.gov/00/staff/pa/cic/money/swindles.txt

33. Hector Tobar, "Victims of Mortgage Scam Home for the Holidays with Benefactor's Aid." *Los Angeles Times*, December 1, 1997.

34. National Futures Association (N.F.A.), Ibid.

35. *Ibid.* The N.F.A. is a Congressionally authorized self-regulatory body financed by the futures industry. Telephone: 1-800-621-3570.

36. *Ibid.*

CHAPTER NINE

❧

VIATORS AND FRAUD:
A WAKE-UP CALL FOR INVESTORS

David E. Wood, Esq.

> How to tell a reckless viatical company from a careful one, how varying state laws can lead to complete loss of principal, and what viatical companies must do to protect investors.

UNTIL THE ADVENT OF VIATICAL SETTLEMENTS, THE TERMINALLY ill person who chose to obtain life insurance by misrepresenting his health had no personal stake in the process.[a] He made what he viewed as a heroic gesture for the exclusive good of his beneficiaries. If he failed to outlive

---

[a] All references to the masculine in this chapter should be deemed to include the feminine as well.

the two-year incontestability period, his martyrdom would be for naught. If, however, he survived this period, then depending on the state in which the policy was issued, his beneficiaries might receive a full death benefit.[1]

This situation carries enormous financial significance for a viatical company and its investors. When a viator obtains a policy by fraud and dies outside the incontestability period, investors will collect the full death benefit notwithstanding the fraud—unless the policy was issued

- ◆ in a state that specifically recognizes some exception to incontestability, or
- ◆ in a state that is faced for the first time with an insurer's request for a judicially-imposed exception to incontestability and grants this request.

For the viatical company, therefore, it is critical to understand how various states treat life insurance policies obtained by fraud when the incontestability period has expired at the time of death.

For the prospective investor, it is critical to ask whether the viatical company monitors—through competent legal counsel—which states allow a fraud exception to incontestability (as well as other key issues affecting whether death benefits ultimately will be paid).

Reckless viatical companies bid on all policies based on uniform percentages. They fail to evaluate the likelihood that some misconduct of the viator will undercut the company's ultimate claim, leaving the investor with nothing.

Careful viatical companies are aware of the different laws of various states and price their settlement bids according to the varying degrees of safety or risk presented by state laws.

COURTS AND INCONTESTABILITY

For more than a century, virtually all life insurance policies have contained incontestability clauses.[2] The clause was mandated by state legislatures that grew weary of long post-mortem battles between insurers and beneficiaries over whether the person whose life was insured lied materially on the application for coverage.

Incontestability laws put insurers on notice that they have two years after a policy is issued to discover irregularities in the application process. After that time, the insurer may not contest coverage once the insured dies.[3]

Incontestability clauses are not intended to condone fraud. Rather, the intent is to establish a time limit within which the question of fraud must be raised.[4] Accordingly, the insurer that agrees to cover a life without an investigation of facts material to the risk does so at its own peril.[5]

DEATH DURING THE INCONTESTABILITY PERIOD

Insurers are free to dispute coverage and may be expected to do so if death occurs during the incontestability period. For example, if the insured stated on the application that he was a non-smoker and then dies of lung cancer within two years, the insurer will take the position that coverage is defeated by the material misrepresentation of the applicant. Thus, the policy will be rendered void *ab initio*.[a]

The heirs may sue the insurer, but after incurring legal expenses they will receive nothing more than a check reimbursing the premiums paid for the policy.

A different issue arises if that same insured dies in an automobile accident—i.e., from a casualty unrelated to his smoking. If the insurer had issued the policy at a higher (smoker) premium, the death benefit would be paid minus the higher premium the insured would have been charged if he had not misrepresented himself.

IMPOSTERS

Several states permit a life insurer to deny coverage where an imposter is substituted for the person insured during the underwriting process. Many other states have not yet addressed the issue. In states where the imposter

---

[a] Ab initio means "from the beginning."

defense is upheld or where the issue has not yet been decided, the purchase of a viator's life insurance policy carries more risk and calls for greater due diligence aimed at unearthing viator fraud committed (but not detected) when the policy was issued.

In jurisdictions that uphold the imposter defense, the facts to which this defense applies are narrow and specific. For the insurer to decline payment the terminally ill person must survive the incontestability period and

1. The terminally ill person must have had an imposter sign the application for life insurance, and

2. The imposter must have appeared for the mandatory medical examination

Under these circumstances, the life insurer agrees to cover the imposter. It is the imposter who signs the necessary documents and causes the policy to be issued. After the terminally ill person dies and his beneficiary submits a claim, the insurer may decline to pay the death claim on the ground that the person who is insured—the imposter—still lives.

Jurisdictions that allow this defense include New York, California, New Jersey, Idaho, Pennsylvania, and Illinois.[6] Some jurisdictions of these courts limit application of the imposter exception to cases in which the imposter posed for the actual insured in all phases of the application and underwriting process.[7] Others allow any misrepresentation (even an innocent one) to defeat coverage after expiration of the contestability period.[8] Some jurisdictions have yet to address the question.

Viatical companies cannot rely upon the life insurer's underwriting when deciding whether or not to buy the viator's policy. In New Jersey, for example, the insurer has no incentive to make certain that the person who applies for coverage and submits to a medical exam is the same person named in the policy. In that state the insurer must pay a claim only upon the death of the person who signed the application and submitted to the medical exam. If the person who signed the application and was examined proves to be someone other than the viator, the life insurer has lost nothing—it simply refunds all premiums paid.

The viatical company faces a very different set of circumstances. If it purchases a policy issued in New Jersey, it assumes a risk the life insurer need not confront: the risk that the viator employed an imposter or made some other misrepresentation in obtaining the policy (intentionally or by mistake, fraudulently or innocently). It is imperative, therefore, for viatical companies doing business in New Jersey to ensure that every material representation made by a viator to obtain coverage is true—and that the person who applied for insurance and the viator are the same.

Legal due diligence must be done by the viatical company before committing to a viatical settlement, and must be done independently of both the life carrier's underwriting and the viatical company's evaluation of the viator's medical condition. If the viatical company discovers fraud only after the viator's death, the viatical settlement proceeds are long gone. Investors will be stuck with an unsalvageable loss.

On the other hand, the life carrier (in New Jersey at least) sustains no loss, provided it discovers fraud before paying the claim on the viator's life. The insurer, therefore, can take action to avoid disaster after the viator's death.

The viatical company has far more at stake in a state like New Jersey at the moment it purchases a viator's policy. If it has not discovered fraud by that time, then the question of whether the claim will be paid and the viatical imposter compensated as agreed will hinge upon the law of the state in which the policy is issued. The viatical company that fails to investigate this law thoroughly exposes its investors to enormous risk.

Great care must be taken to anticipate the ways in which an apparently iron-clad law can be overturned, rendering the value of the viatical company's interest in a purchased policy uncertain.

Consider the situation in California. In 1935 that state's legislature imposed a two-year incontestability period upon all group life insurance and added the clause by statute to all individual policies in 1974. Through the years California courts have held that once the incontestability period expires, the death benefit is payable regardless of whether the insured obtained the policy by fraud.[9]

In a case decided early in 1997, the California Supreme Court upheld the state's traditional prohibition. It ruled against the insurer who raised fraud after an insured's death, since death occurred after the incontestability period expired.[10]

In that case the viator discovered he was HIV-positive, applied for life insurance in his own name and signed the application himself but had a healthy imposter take the required blood test and medical examination. Later, the viator sold the policy to a viatical company.

The insurer learned of the fraud and denied the viatical company's claim for payment of the death benefit. Litigation ensued. The insurer asked the trial court to enter summary judgment upholding its denial of coverage on the ground that the person it agreed to insure was not the viator, but the imposter. The trial court denied this motion, the court of appeal affirmed, and the California Supreme Court granted review.

The supreme court agreed with the viatical company. Holding that the insurer and the insured had reached an agreement as to the identity of the person whose life would be covered, the court ruled that the carrier had contracted to insure not the person whose blood was tested but the person who signed the application.

Under this circumstance, the court held that the medical examination was a fraud . . . the insurer could not raise as a defense to coverage by virtue of the expired incontestability period. Because the viator, not the imposter, signed the application for insurance, the claim was payable to the viatical company.

What is critically important about this decision is not what it held but what it did not hold. The court did not rule out affording the life insurer an imposter defense where the imposter, not the viator, actually signed the application. Had this occurred, the Court strongly suggested, it would have ruled for the life insurer. The viator's fraud would have been an absolute defense to payment of the claim.

It seems unlikely that the viatical company performed a handwriting analysis of the viator's signature before purchasing his policy. The fact that the viatical company probably left this pivotal factor entirely to chance illustrates the importance of non-medical due diligence in the decision whether to purchase a particular policy—even in a jurisdiction like California which, before 1997, seemed a safe state for the viatical business.

CONCLUSION

Viatical companies must perform a thorough medical evaluation of the viator to accurately gauge his life expectancy, but it is no less important to determine if the laws of the state in which the policy was issued will enforce payment of death benefits when the claim is presented.

To do this, viatical companies must determine which incontestability period applies to the policy. The viatical company also should obtain the opinion of competent legal counsel as to whether changes in state law afford the insurer a basis for contesting coverage.

In California, for example, it is now critical for the viatical company to verify that the viator is the person whose signature appears on the insurance application. Different states will have different criteria that warrant specific attention during the viatical company's risk evaluation process.

If the viatical company cannot show that it devotes the necessary resources to learning the law of each state so as to evaluate the risk of doing business there, it is gambling with its investors' funds.

END NOTES

1. Timed incontestability is a unique feature of life and disability insurance. With any other kind of insurance the insurer may raise the insured's material misrepresentation or concealment of a material fact as a defense to coverage when a claim is made, and may also sue to rescind the policy upon discovery of fraud—whenever that occurs. *See* e.g., California Insurance § 330 et seq. Accordingly, for policies other than life and disability, the applicant's misrepresentation or concealment of a material fact on which the insurer justifiably relies to its detriment, will void coverage.

2. California Insurance Code § 10206, enacted in 1935, requires a two-year incontestability period for group life insurance policies. California Insurance Code § 10113.5, enacted in 1974, establishes the same period for individual policies.

3. In *Northwestern Mutual Life Insurance Company v. Johnson,* 254 U.S. 96, 101-102, 41 S.Ct. 47, 49, 65 L.Ed. 155 (1920), the United States Supreme Court noted the purpose behind the incontestability clause:

> The object of the clause is plain and laudable—to create an absolute assurance of the benefit, as free as may be from any dispute of fact except the fact of death, and as soon as it reasonably can be done.

4. *Dibble v. Reliance Life Insurance Company* (1915) 170 Cal. 199, 208.

5. In *Amex Life Assurance Company v. Superior Court* (Slome Capital Corporation) (1997) 14 Cal.4th 1231, 1234, the California Supreme Court articulated the rationale behind the incontestability clause:

> As early as 1915, this court described this type of incontestability clause—now required by statute in all group and individual life insurance policies—as "'in the nature of . . . statutes of limitation and repose . . . .' (Dibble v. Reliance Life Ins. Co. (1915) 170 Cal. 199, 209, 149 P.171; see, Insurance Code §§ 10113.5, 10206.) After the premiums have been paid and the insured has survived for two years, the insurance company may not contest coverage even if the insured committed fraud in applying for the policy. The incontestability clause, we have explained, "is not a stipulation absolutely to waive all defenses and to condone fraud. On the contrary, it recognizes fraud and all other defenses but it provides ample time and opportunity within which they may be, but beyond which they may not be, established." (<u>Dibble</u>, supra, 170 Cal. 209, 149 P. 171.)

END NOTES

6. *Maslin v. Columbian National Life Insurance Company*, 3 F.Supp. 368 (S.D.N.Y. 1932) [finding an imposter exception to the incontestability clause]; *Berkshire Life Insurance Company v. Owens*, 910 F. Supp. 132 (S.D.N.Y. 1996) ["the incontestability clause permits the carrier to deny coverage on the ground of fraud without regard to time"]; *Ludwinska v. John Hancock Mutual Life Insurance Company* (Pa. 1935) 577, 178 A. 28 [upholding an imposter defense to incontestability]; *Petacccio v. New York Life Insurance Company* (Pa. App. 1937) 125 Pa.Super. 15, 189 A. 697 [upholding an imposter defense]; *Amex Life Assurance Company v. Superior Court (Slome Capital Corporation)* (Cal. 1997) 14 Cal.4th 123 [suggesting that true imposter exception to incontestability would be upheld]; *Valant v. Metropolitan Life Insurance Company* (Ill. App. 1939) 302 Ill. App. 196, 23 N.E.2d 922 [upholding imposter defense]; *Obartuch v. Security Mutual Life Insurance Company, 114 F.2d 873* (7th Cir. 1940) [upholding imposter defense]; cf *Maxwell v. Cumberland Life Insurance Company* (Idaho 1987) 113 [describing imposter exception]; *Fioretti v. Massachusetts General Life Insurance Company* (11th Cir. 1995) 53 F.3d affirming *Fioretti v. Massachusetts General Life Insurance Company* (S.D. Fla. 1993) 892 F.Supp. 1492 [holding, under New Jersey law, that a life insurer may rescind coverage after expiration of the incontestability period on the ground of material misrepresentation—even when it is innocently made]; *Strawbridge v. New York Life Insurance Company* 504 F. Supp. 824 (D.N.J. 1980) [upholding defense to coverage based upon misrepresentation after expiration of the incontestability period, in the absence of fraud].

7. See e.g., *Maslin v. Columbian National Life Insurance Company*, 3 F.Supp. 368 (S.D.N.Y. 1932); *Ludwinska v. John Hancock Mutual Life Insurance Company* (Pa. 1935) 577, 178 A. 28; *Amex Life Assurance Company v. Superior Court (Slome Capital Corporation)* (Cal. 1997) 14 Cal.4th 1231.

8. *Fioretti v. Massachusetts*, supra; *Strawbridge v. New York Life*, supra.

9. *United Fidelity Life Insurance Company v. Emert* (1996) 49 Cal. App.4th 941, 945-46 [where the insured misrepresented on the application that he was not HIV-positive, and concealed the identity of the doctor treating this condition, expiration of the contestability period prevented the life insurer from denying coverage based on the fraud].

10. *Amex Life Assurance Company v. Superior Court* (Slome Capital Corporation), supra.

CHAPTER TEN

❖

WEALTHY
OR WANNABE?

Viatical investments may prove to be a road paved with gold. They may be, as many believe, a unique opportunity, the chance of a lifetime. But this investment is not suitable for everyone. Here are a few tools to help you evaluate whether it is suitable for you.

D O YOU HAVE $200 THOUSAND TO INVEST? IF SO, AND IF YOUR net worth is one million dollars, you qualify for viatical investments sponsored by Affirmative Lifestyles Viatical Funding, Inc. (ALI).[a]

ALI, an investment partnership, is unique to the viatical industry. The

---

[a] The securities law under which ALI operates prohibits advertising. Details are presented here for informational purposes only. Do not construe this as either an encouragement or an advertisement.

general partners, Peggy and Tom Wallace, are strict about compliance with existing securities laws. To date, ALI is the only viatical investment company that openly declares the states in which it has applied for and received exemption from the securities laws.[a]

In order to participate in ALI's program, investors must qualify by certain financial standards. Although the other viatical companies accept anyone's money, they require investors to sign a statement attesting that they are "sophisticated" investors and "suitable" for this investment. Some also include a declaration that the investor understands the risks or has the advice of a financial professional and/or enough funds for living expenses and emergencies.

So, are you a suitable investor for viatical settlement contracts?

THE SUITABLE INVESTOR

One viatical investment company, LifeLine, describes the suitable investor as one who

> can bear the economic risk of a purchase of Benefits; has adequate means of providing for his/her current needs and possible contingencies; and has no need for liquidity of his/her funds or the Benefits.

LifeLine also requires investors to attest that

> He/She is committing him/herself to a purchase which bears a reasonable relationship to his/her net worth.[b]

These are general principles and they apply to consideration of any investment. Answers should not be wishful thinking nor rough estimates. Before committing a sum of money investors should give themselves a financial "checkup." This means you should evaluate the following:

---

[a] Pages x-x of ALI's prospectus.

[b] Page 2 of LifeLine's agency agreement.

- Monthly cash flow: After all expenses, do you have cash left over?
- Emergency funds. Do you have cash/sufficient liquidity for six months of expenses if you lose your job or incur major home repair costs or medical expense?
- Insurance. Do you have adequate medical, disability, life, and auto insurance to protect yourself and your loved ones?
- Debts. Are you carrying too much debt, especially credit card debt?
- Goals. Have you determined your short- and long-term goals? This is important since different goals require different investment strategies.
- Risk tolerance. Have you determined your tolerance for risk?
- Investments. If you have other investments, do they match your goals? risk tolerance? Are they diversified?

Note: If these questions cause you to feel uneasy, stop here and consult a financial planner. Don't make any investment decisions before you free yourself of obligations that should take priority.

LIQUIDITY

Liquid investments are readily converted to cash. If a sales agent tells you this is a liquid investment, ask how much his company would pay you tomorrow if you had to sell the contract you buy today.

> Without both liquidity and marketability, there is no flexibility. Liquidity is the measure of the investors' ability to turn all or most of his investment back into cash. Marketability is a measure of the speed and ease at which a buyer (through sale, trade, or otherwise) can dispose of his investment.[1]

One reason that viaticals are not liquid is that, at this writing, there is no *legitimate* secondary market. That is not to say that none exists. Since everyone wants to be part of this booming industry, there are a few new companies that specialize in resales. But there are problems with resales.

Viaticals are resold at fire sale prices. The secondary buyer gets a bargain and the broker who finds the secondary buyer gets a fee, as does the escrow company that holds the funds until the transaction is completed. Sellers bear all expenses—new escrow fees, premiums, etc.

If you must resell, don't be quick to sell to the same viatical company that handled the initial transaction. Check costs with other viatical companies. They may offer a better deal if they have investors waiting for policies. Put the law of supply and demand to work for you.

If you are offered a viatical investment in the secondary market, you may be told that you are getting a bargain, that the viator is closer to death than when the initial investor bought the policy. This may seem like "too good to be true" but you don't know which claims to challenge. Keep in mind: All the risks that apply to initial buyers apply to secondary buyers, as well.

SAFETY

Viaticals are promoted for safety of principal. They *are* safe—if the sale is legal, if the insurer doesn't become insolvent, if the policy remains in force until the insured's demise, and if the viator doesn't disappear. Then every dollar of your investment will be returned.

If you're concerned about maturity risk and the possibility of paying premiums indefinitely, you may be tempted by the surety bond offered by a few maverick companies, including the one salesman Mal represents.[a] Unfortunately, at this writing the surety bonds for viatical investments aren't offered by any company that could be considered reliable.

CURRENT INCOME

Investments that pay interest or dividends provide current income. A few new companies offer monthly annuity income during the period between purchase of the investment and the demise of the insured. Following are a few of the more worrisome aspects of this offer:

♦ The insurance laws of all states restrict annuity sales to insurance companies and banks.

---

[a] Details about the surety bond are in chapter 4, "Signing Up."

- At this writing, none of the companies that make this offer are licensed to buy policies from viators.
- Since viatical companies often have cash flow problems, one has to wonder about the source of this income stream.

One company explained the source of the annuity-like income was unpaid broker commissions (e.g., commissions that are not paid until the policy matures). However, it seems unlikely that brokers would be willing to wait years to be paid for their work.

INFLATION

Viaticals may be a very good inflation hedge since they have potential for very high returns.

YIELD

It's possible to have huge profits from this investment, but it's also possible that the sales agent is misleading investors. Yield is effected by how many years the viator lives past life expectancy, and if premiums must be paid by investors. Yield may also be effected if funds sit in escrow for a period of time. Mutual Benefits Corporation of Florida, described earlier, were accused by the SEC of selling more than $100 million worth of unregistered securities to more than 1,190 investors nationwide, and misleading the investors about their rate of return.[a]

The charge of misleading investors was based primarily on the rate of return being reduced from the start, when funds were held in MBC's checking account for several weeks before being placed on a policy.[2]

Leslie Stringer, president, director, and sole shareholder of Mutual Benefits, and his brother Joel Steinger, the co-founder of Mutual Benefits, agreed to a judgment that permanently bars them from violating the registration and anti-fraud provisions of federal securities laws. Additionally,

---

[a] Chapter 8, "Fraud Watch," page 131.

they were forced to refund or exchange investor funds involved in the sale of these policies, surrender $850,000 in earnings and interest, and pay $50,000 each in civil penalties.[3]

TAX CONSEQUENCES

Many viatical companies tell investors something like this:

> Keep in mind. Life Insurance companies are exempt from the 1099 form filing requirements normally associated with the payment of funds to beneficiaries. Therefore, the payment of tax by an investor in a viatical settlement is done on a voluntary basis.[a]

What happens if you don't "volunteer" to report and pay tax on the gain? If you don't report the gain and pay the tax that is due, you are guilty of tax evasion. This is not tax avoidance, a legal method whereby tax law is used to avoid tax. Tax evasion is fraud. You may get away with it today. You may not be found out for years, but there is no statute of limitations on fraud.

Sales promoters may be right when they claim that the IRS won't find out about your investment gain. But if they're right, this investment will become very attractive to criminals who seek avenues for money laundering. And when that happens, the IRS will launch an intensive money-hunt, starting with audits of insurance companies—to find beneficiaries of policies that were viaticated. Then they will audit viatical companies—to collect lists of investors who were paid by these companies.

Since the purpose of this book is to help you invest safely, don't risk the consequences of tax fraud. Report and pay tax on the gain.

Gain from viatical investments is based on the "cost recovery rule." This means you are taxed on the amount you receive, after subtracting (recovering) the cost of the investment.

However, it's possible that you will be taxed on an amount greater than the death benefit. If you receive interest earned on cash values, this interest is

---

[a] Page 7 of LifeLine's brochure.

taxable—even if you didn't directly receive it but had the insurer apply the interest to the purchase of additional death benefits.

There is no tax due on dividends from a mutual life insurance company since these dividends are considered a return of excess premiums and are not taxable. Also non-taxable are refunds of unearned premiums, since these premiums were paid with after-tax dollars.[4]

If you're in a high tax bracket and used viatical investments for a qualified retirement trust (QRT), you won't pay taxes until funds are withdrawn from the qualified plan. Then the same tax reporting rules apply as for other investments withdrawn from a QRT.

You probably can use viaticals for Keoghs, defined contribution or defined benefits plans—but don't go within ten feet of putting IRA funds into viaticals until the Internal Revenue Code is changed, or viaticals are declared securities by the federal government.

IRA FUNDS

By law, no part of IRA trust funds may be invested in life insurance.[5] Yet most mavericks and a number of legitimate companies urge investors to do so and they provide forms to make it simple. Additionally, investors are misled by claims that viatical investments are "approved" or "suitable" for IRAs.

> The truth is there is no such thing as an `IRA Approved' or `sanctioned' investment. The IRS *does not give its blessing to specific investments.*[6] [sic]

Since this is a self-directed IRA, if the IRS audits you, you can't point a finger at the viatical company, its escrow agent, or the IRA custodian.

> IRA funds must be handled by a custodian, such as a bank, trust department or mutual fund. However the custodian of IRA funds is not obligated to review or approve of the investments selected for self-directed IRA.[7]

This may come as a shock to those of you who already invested viaticals in your IRA. The forms looked exactly like the ones you used for other Individual Retirement Accounts. That made the IRA seem legitimate.

However, investment choices are not the responsibility of IRA trustees. Nor are they required to give advice. They are, in effect, bookkeepers. If you want to invest in extraterrestrial spaceships or cotton candy or magic rocks, IRA trustees could keep the books for your investment and never say a word.

This is equally true of IRA trustees employed by national banks. Yet nothing precludes an investor from asking advice of bank trust officers. For example, Northern Trust Bank of Florida holds the custodial account for at least one viatical company. If investors asked second vice president Marian L. Hasty about viaticals and IRAs, they would hear this:[8]

> IRAs have a strict prohibition against investing in life insurance policies. Until the issue of whether these investments are insurance products or securities like stocks or bonds is resolved, we believe they should not be purchased for IRAs.

Investors should—but don't—read the small print in the IRA brochure. The warning is there, as required by law. For example, Retirement Accounts, Inc. (RAI), which services the IRA program for a number of viatical companies, includes the following a disclosure statement entitled "Statutory Requirements."

No part of the custodial funds may be invested in life insurance.[a]

Some viatical companies base their offer of IRAs on dicta from the appeals court that ruled on the SEC-Life Partners case: Viatical investments are not life insurance.[9] Some viatical companies take it a step farther and apply a tactic devised by Life Partners to get around the IRS prohibition. In this tactic the IRA lends funds to a trust (or to the viatical company). As described by the appeals court:

---

[a] Page 8 of 11 pages in RAI's "Disclosure Statement."

> In order to circumvent the Internal Revenue Code prohibition upon IRAs investing in life insurance contracts, LPI structures the purchase through a separate trust established for that purpose. The IRA lends money to the trust, for which it receives a non-recourse note; the trust then uses the loan proceeds to purchase an interest in a life insurance policy, the death benefits of which collateralize the note.
> When the insured dies and the benefits are paid, the proceeds go to pay off the note held by the IRA.[10]

One of the legitimate companies that follows this model, Dedicated Resources, explains it this way: [a]

> The LENDER hereby agrees to lend the sum of ___ USD, ($) to ___ in return for a non-recourse note secured by Irrevocable Beneficiary interest in a Viatical Settlement Policy or Policies having a face value of ___ USD ($___) upon maturity.
> The note shall be discharged and deemed paid in full when the LENDER receives death benefits in the sum of ____ USD ($___) from ___ Insurance Company at policy maturity. The note shall be non-recourse and LENDER shall look solely to the Proceeds of life insurance policy(ies) assigned as collateral for payment of sums due.[b]

In other words, the IRA lends money to the trust or viatical company which does the actual investing. Is an IRA loan a better method for getting around the IRS's prohibition? No.

> If any part of an individual retirement account is used by the individual as security for a loan, that portion is deemed distributed on the first day of the tax year in which the loan was made.[11]

And penalties are steep. According to James Bone, CPA, the IRA loan may be viewed as a premature distribution. As such, it would be subject to income tax plus penalties for premature distribution:

---

[a] In this instance the investor is referred to as "Lender" and Dedicated Resources is the "Debtor."

[b] Page 1, number 1, sections1.1 and 1.2 of Dedicated Resources IRA Funding Agreement.

10 percent of the amount involved in the prohibited transaction for
each year the transaction is open, plus a potential 100% tax on the
amount involved.[a]

If this arrangement were to be deemed legal at some future date, a
multitude of tax-related questions will need answers. For example, since "the
Lender may be required to add funds" if the premium reserve account is
depleted, will additional premiums be considered IRA contributions or IRA
maintenance fees? [b]

We asked Mal, the salesman mentioned earlier, how life insurance
proceeds are handled in this arrangement. He said that death benefits are paid
to the individual, not to the IRA. Then the individual can choose to reinvest
these funds in the IRA. He didn't explain how this suddenly large amount
could be reinvested when there is a $2,000 limit on annual contributions to an
IRA.

Legacy Capital did not immediately offer IRAs. They were concerned
about the legalities. After researching how this may be done they designed a
plan whereby the escrow agent is named as owner of the policy. Thus the
escrow agent, not the investor, has control over the policy. The investor's IRA
simply invests in the death benefits.

Legacy felt comfortable in proceeding with this plan after its paperwork
was reviewed by the IRA custodian, Pensco, a San Francisco company that has
been in business for years and handles many IRAs for viatical companies. A
phone call to the legal department at Pensco yielded this explanation: Viatical
contracts are not life insurance; they are investments. Pensco refused to
acknowledge that this was a gray area of tax law, or that related issues remain
unresolved. Among them:

♦ If the investor's intent is to use IRA funds to invest in life insurance,
will the tax court's decision rest on "intent" to commit tax fraud?

---

[a] Ibid.

[b] Page 2, article three, number 2 of Dedicated Resources IRA Funding Agreement.

- If policy ownership is turned over to an escrow agent, is this a "premature distribution" of the IRA?
- What rule applies if ownership is turned over to the escrow agent for no consideration (i.e., no money is exchanged)?

Warning: These questions should make it clear that investors ought not to place viatical investments in their self-directed IRAs unless they have consulted a knowledgeable tax professional.

END NOTES

1. Stephen R. Leimberg, J.D., CLU; Martin J. Satinsky, CPA, J.D., LL.M.; Robert T. LeClair, Ph.D. *The Tools and Techniques of Financial Planning*, 2d edition, 1987. National Underwriter, Cincinnati, Ohio.

2. SEC v. Joel Steinger and Leslie Steinger. *SEC News Digest*, May 4, 1998. Available: gov.us.fed.sec.announce.

3. "Mutual Benefits Founders Settle SEC Complaints." *Reuters News Service*, and *America Online News Service*, May 7, 1998.

4. An unearned premium occurs when premiums are paid in advance and the insured dies or cancels a policy during the premium period.

5. *Tax Facts 1*, National Underwriter Company. (Cincinnati, Ohio, 1997). Also, IRC § 408(a)(3)25 and IRS Publication 590.

6. Colorado Securities Administrator Philip A. Feigin, past-president of the North American Securities Administrators Association (NASAA), quoted in "Bogus `IRA Approved' Investment Schemes." Published by NASAA. Available: http://www.nasaa.org/investoredu/investoralerts/bogusira.html.

7. *Ibid.*

8. Marian L. Hasty, J.D., *"What Does `Viatical' Mean?"* Ms. Hasty, a vice president of Northern Trust Bank, Miami, Florida, is a cum laude graduate of the University of Miami School of Law, has an LL.M. in estate planning, and currently works in the Trust Business Development Department. Available at http://www.ntrs.com/pfs/mny596.html.

9. ". . . a viatical settlement is not an insurance policy, and the business of selling fractional interests in insurance policies is no part of `the business of insurance.'" *Securities and Exchange Commission, Appellee v. Life Partners, Incorporated and Brian D. Pardo, Appellants*, No. 95-5364, United States Court of Appeals for the District of Columbia Circuit, July 5, 1996, Decided.

10. *Ibid.*

11. Tax Facts, *Ibid..*

CHAPTER ELEVEN

❖

CONCLUSION

R EMEMBER MAL, THE VIATICAL SALES AGENT/INSURANCE
agent/stockbroker? During our first phone contact I asked about
the companies he represented. Mal said, "We have two that buy
policies from brokers who bought from the individuals who sold them."

Mal should have read "Cash for the Final Days." Then he would know
that brokers don't buy policies from viators. That is, *licensed* viatical brokers
don't buy policies.

Mal went on to say that yield definitely is guaranteed at 30 percent
through a surety bond available to investors who buy "36-month paper." If
the viator lives past 36 months, the surety bond pays principal plus 30 percent
interest. There is a drawback, however. Investors who take the risk instead of
the surety bond may get a yield as high as 80 percent, if the viator dies early.
With the surety bond, yield is locked in at 30 percent.

How much does the bond cost? Nothing. Then how does the company
make a profit? No answer.

Here's my guess. The process starts with the company that offers the surety bond—a marketing company set up for the purpose of marketing viatical contracts to investors. Their sales agent gets a commission, the marketing company gets a commission, and the viatical company that initially bought the policy takes its profit. After paying that queue, how much of the investor's purchase funds are paid to viators?

The first possibility is that these viators didn't know they should apply to several funding firms so that they could sell their policies to the highest bidder. If the viators had only one purchase offer, they surely were paid thousands of dollars less than they otherwise would have received.

The second scenario takes more from investors. It may work this way: A viator's life expectancy is estimated at 48 months, and the viator is paid accordingly. But investors are told that life expectancy is 24 months. Since shorter life expectancies mean higher purchase prices, investors pay more. The additional dollars pay commissions and the cost of the surety bond. If the policy doesn't "mature" after 36 months, the investor is paid through the surety bond.

The next scenario uses the surety bond to deceive viators as well as investors. The company selects a viator who applied to no other company, someone with a short life expectancy, perhaps twelve months. The investor buys a 12-months life expectancy and the viator is paid for a 36-months life expectancy.[a] When the viator dies within one year, the investor gets the additional 30 percent guaranteed by the surety bond, but not the 100 or 150 percent yield actually earned. That bonus goes into the coffers of the viatical and marketing companies.

This scenario is hypothetical, of course. Mal assured us that none of his clients had opted for the "Trust," which is the plan with the surety bond.

The sales pitch is enthusiastic, but one has to wonder: If this investment

[a] Viators usually are not told their life expectancies, nor given any other disclosures about the financing of their policies. Residents of Washington are an exception since that state's viatical regulation requires these disclosures.

truly is a wealth builder, why does this guy run around days, nights, week ends, and in Mal's case dragging a portable televison hooked up to a VCR so that he can show the much-touted segment of 60 minutes in which several years ago news anchor Morley Safer heaped praised on this new industry. The segment we were shown also featured Brian Pardo and Life Partners, Inc., although Mal claims not to be selling for Life Partners.[a]

Why not? Because they're not quick enough at processing investor orders. Mal's reply made no reference to the Cease and Desist Orders issued by the California Department of Insurance in 1996 against Life Partners and Brian Pardo.

When asked how low the purchase price might go, Mal said, "Whatever the market will bear."

My friend then asked, "Are there any laws regarding viatical settlements?"

This salesman who claims to have 22 years as a licensed life insurance and annuity agent and stockbroker said: "No."

No? He didn't know that California was the first state to enact viatical regulation to protect viators? He was unaware that the Department of Corporations considers the sale of fractionalized shares to be securities?

Mal also seemed unaware that licensed insurance agents are prohibited from using the state guarantee fund as a sales tool. Perhaps he didn't care; or perhaps he assumed investors wouldn't know.

Mal is typical of an increasing number of life insurance agents, financial planners, and securities brokers who are involved in viatical sales. One company boasts of years as a licensed securities dealer; it offers viatical investments in affiliation with Life Partners, Incorporated. Others, individuals who claim to be registered securities brokers, brag about viaticals to investment groups on the Internet. Each parrots the claim, "Wall Street would not touch this with a 10-foot pole and yet it's 10 times better than anything

---

[a] The program aired in 1995. Pardo was interviewed—not held up as an icon of the industry.

Wall Street has in fixed income investments." [a]

Lawyers have begun to act as viatical investment brokers. One claims that the proceeds of this investment are tax-free to purchasers. This lawyer bases his claim on a unique interpretation of the Health Care Accountability and Portability Act of 1996.[1] To date it has been impossible to find another tax or legal professional who supports this interpretation.

Now banks are getting into the act.[2] At this writing at least three banks offer viatical investments provided by funding firm, Dedicated Resources.[3] This coup for Dedicated Resources is the result of enlisting "25-year marketing veteran Alan Blank," who then set up Midwood Financial Services, Inc., in Encino, California and went to work selling viaticals to banks.[4]

One of these banking clients is First Merit Bank of Akron, Ohio, described as a "supercommunity bank" (with more than a dozen branches in Akron). First Merit offers viatical investments in minimum amounts of $10,000, and there is an unconfirmed report of a single investment at First Merit in the amount of $500,000. According to First Merit's broker/dealer prsident, Felice Larmer, "The icome is tax-free since the investor actually owns the discounted life insruance policy." [5]

Was it Blank who told First Merit that this investment was tax-free? Or did he tell them, as reported to the Bank Mutual Fund Report,

> If a viator sells his or her policy, the proceeds are tax free. However the proceeds to the buyer are not.

When faced with such contradictory statements, what should investors believe? Consider the source or, as they say in the trenches, "Follow the Money." If a statement emanates from someone who profits from the sale of this investment—and that includes bank officials— take the statement (and the sales materials) with a hefty dose of cynicism.

The viatical industry is beset with lies, half-truths, and misinformation. It's

---

[a] Quoted exactly.

unfortunate and it's unnecessary. The industry is booming. It's exploding across the borders of the U.S. into Canada, to the U.K., to Germany, to Australia, to Asia. This is due primarily to the Internet, and the furious marketing by viatical companies of all stripes.

Moreover, the appearance of print advertisements in respectable newspapers such as The Los Angeles Times and Investors' Business Daily indicate that viatical settlements, while still relatively unknown to most people, are becoming mainstream.

As a result, investors will continue to be drawn to viatical settlement contracts. Some will be harmed, primarily those who are uninformed about investments in general and viaticals in particular, and those who are eager to believe that huge returns are possible without risk.

Lacking regulation, viatical companies make their own rules. Legitimate companies mimic the mavericks as much as the mavericks mimic them. Securities regulation is one way to protect investors and, ultimately, the industry. As federal circuit judge Patricia Wald noted in her argument for regulation of the viatical industry,

> The design of the statutes is to protect investors by promoting full disclosure of information thought necessary to informed investor decisions. This need for information holds true in regard to investors prior to purchase as much as to investors who have committed their funds—indeed, more so, if they are to avoid over-risky investments.[6]

Federal regulation may not come about for some years, not until there are sufficient numbers of investor lawsuits to make regulation imperative. Meanwhile, increasing numbers of states are taking action against companies that offer fractionalized shares of viatical contracts but are not registered as securities dealers and have not registered the investment as a security. Often these companies commit fraud and misrepresentation, as well. However, state regulation is in in its infancy. The officials in charge will soon discover the necessity to coordinate their efforts with those of other states.

Texans, for example, lost several thousands when they invested with a now-defunct Alabama-based viatical company. The successors to the Alabama company were the subjects of Cease and Desist Orders issued by Missouri.[a]

A Minnesota farm couple placed their life's savings with a Florida-based company and lost 12.5 percent.

California investor lost his entire IRA when he invested it with a Texas-based company.

Residents of twenty-four states were victims of the Ponzi scheme perpetrated by Personal Choice Opportunities.[b]

Regulation is a partial remedy. Regulation prescribes certain rules, but enforcement tends to be reactive—after investors are harmed. Proactive measures are needed to ensure investor safety and the continuity of the viatical industry. This will occur if financial professionals are willing to exercise their power.[c]

The power of financial professionals is through their clients' dollars— thousands, perhaps millions of investor dollars they can bring to viatical companies. This gives financial professionals the power to refuse to do business with any company that won't fully disclose all risks and all expenses, and that won't change its contract to provide better protection for clients.

Financial professionals have a choice: either stay out of the industry or get in and earn good commissions. If they get in, they must perform due diligence or their clients' funds will be at risk and so will their own licenses and, ultimately, their careers.[7] Imagine the impact of these demands on the viatical industry. In order to be competitive, the mavericks will be forced to disclose risks and revise contracts, too.

If we keep investors safe, the industry will remain viable. If we keep investors safe, the industry will continue its phenomenal growth. If we make

---

[a] See appendix VII.

[b] Detailed in chapter 8, "Fraud Watch."

[c] Licensed financial professionals include N.A.S.D. registered representatives, licensed insurance agents, attornesy, accountants, financial planners.

these efforts today, thousands of patients in the decades to come will benefit. They will be able to die with dignity because informed and caring investors gave them cash for the final days.

END NOTES

1. Steven J. Kaufman, J.D., C.L.U., C.P.C.U., F.L.M.I, C.E.P.P., and Bonnie L. Kaufman, L.U.T.C., C.E.P.P. "Using Viatical Settlements in Retirement and Estate Planning." *Life Insurance Selling*, April, 1998, St. Louis, Missouri.

2. Amy S. Friedman, "Banks Now Selling Viatical Settlements." *National Underwriter*, Life and Health-Financial Services edition, November 3, 1997.

3. Premium Federal Savings Bank of Gibbsboro, New Jersey is another bank that markets viaticals provided by Dedicated Resources. Premium F.S.B. states that "viatical settlements can be purchased with qualified money. They are a natural investment for your retirement assets." Available: www.premium.com/viatical.htm.

4. Friedman, *Ibid.*

5. "First Merit Weighs in with Viaitcal Program." *Bank Mutual Fund Report*, November 3, 1997. Available: www.northernlight.com.

6. J. Patricia Wald's dissent to *Securities and Exchange Commission, Appellee, v. Life Partners, Incorporated and Brian D. Pardo, Appellants*, No. 95-5364, Decided July 5, 1996.

7. Financial professionals can be held accountable. The Wall Street Journal regularly posts punitive actions imposed by the regulatory arm of the National Association of Securities Dealers (NASD). One type of complaint that is met with harshly is when brokers make investment recommendations "without reasonable grounds for believing they would be suitable for the customer."

Appendices

Figures from an Actual Insurer Insolvency
Prepared by Jack Traylor, DPA (see Chapter 7, "Belly-up" Insurance)

Owner Name	State	Policy Value	Policy Count	Less CA Coinsurance	Policy Value Less Coinsurance	State Limit	Non-Covered Amount
XXX	AR	$254,000	20	0	$254,000	$100,000	$154,500
XXX	CA	$143,011	4	$28,602	$114,409	$100,000	$ 14,409
XXX	CA	$190,000	4	$38,046	$152,183	$100,000	$ 52,183
XXX	CO	$382,392	1	0	$382,392	$100,000	$ 282,392
XXX	FL	$248,672	2	0	$248,672	$100,000	$ 148,672
XXX	FL	$100,140	1	0	$100,140	$100,000	$ 140
XXX	NE	$307,083	2	0	$307,083	$100,000	$207,083
XXX	TX	$ 99,000	9	0	$ 99,000	$100,000	0

Appendix I: Assumption Document

Group Policies: Special Risks[1]

A. **Insured Returns to Full Time Work: Same Employer**

If an insured who is on disability premium waiver returns to work full time with the existing employer, one of two possibilities will occur:

1. Employer remained with the same Insurance Carrier

   a. Insured's Group Interest[b] is protected; however, premiums may become due on the Group Interest.

   b. ABC may become responsible for ongoing insurance premiums in order to maintain such Group Interest.

2. Employer Changed Insurance Carriers since the date ABC acquired the Group Interest

   a. The Group Interest with the prior carrier will terminate.

   b. There is no assurance ABC will be an assignee under any new Master Policy.

   c. ABC will have to obtain Assignment of the Insured's Group Interest in

---

[1] Adapted from underwriting guidelines of Accelerated Benefits Capital, Inc., which has offices in Michigan and Montreal.

[b] Group Insurance is issued under a Master Policy, which is owned by the Employer. Thus, the Master Policy continues or terminates based on decisions of the Employer and/or the insurance carrier.

the new Master Policy.

d. The Insured will be contractually obligated to assign his/her rights under the new Master Policy to ABC or its designee (see "Agreement in the Event of Change of Insurance Coverage" document).[a]

e. The Insured's Employer and the Employer's insurance carrier will be notified of the Insured's obligation to ABC. However, there is no assurance that either one will honor this without the Insured's cooperation.

f. In addition, there is no assurance that a new Master Policy with a new insurance carrier will provide the same amount of coverage as the old Master Policy.

g. If the death benefit under the new Master Policy is less, the Insured will be required to obtain sufficient additional insurance from the Employer to make up the shortfall, if such option is available. [b]

h. Premiums for additional insurance will be the responsibility of ABC.

i. If there is no option to acquire

---

[a] The "Agreement" form is not included here.

[b] Many employer group plans provide a specified amount of life insurance at no cost to employees, but may allow employees to buy additional insurance at their own expense.

additional insurance, upon the death
of the Insured ABC will receive a
lower net death benefit from the new
Master Policy.

j. ABC sends notices signed by the
Insured to the insurance carrier and
Employer to request that ABC receive
copies of all notices or changes
concerning the Master Policy.
However, there is no assurance either
the insurer or the Employer will
comply with these notices.

B. **Insured Returns to Work: New Employer**

1. ABC will have to obtain an Assignment of
the Master Policy with a new Employer
(see "Agreement in the Event of Change of
Insurance Coverage" document).[a]

2. The aforementioned risks apply to this
event.

C. **Risks Concerning Disability Premium Waivers**

1. Most insurance company disability premium
waivers are reviewed on a periodic basis,
usually annually.

2. Updated medical information must be
provided to show continuing disability.

3. In some cases Insureds must sign forms to
request renewal of the disability waiver.

4. If the waiver is not renewed and the

---

[a] This form is not provided here.

Insured does not return to work, the Insured's Group Interest may terminate.

a. To continue coverage, the Policy will have to be converted to a permanent Policy.

b. In such case, premiums will be due on the Policy, and these will be the responsibility of ABC.

c. If the conversion is to a whole life or universal life policy, such premiums can be significant.[a]

d. While ABC receives a special Power of Attorney[b] from the insured to grant ABC the power to renew disability premium waivers, many insurance companies insist on the signature of the Insured or the Insured's physician.

e. There is no assurance that ABC will be able to obtain the signature of the Insured or the Insured's physician for a disability premium waiver renewal.

f. If the waiver is not renewed, ABC has the power to convert the policy under its special Power of Attorney.

g. Premiums will have to be paid on the Policy until the death of the Insured.

---

[a] Group term insurance premiums may be $200 a year; conversion premiums for the same amount may be ten times greater, depending on the age of the insured and the face amount.

[b] This form is not provided here.

D. **Employer Changes Insurance Carriers While Insured is on Disability Waiver**
    1. Due to the disability premium waiver, the Insured's Group Interest stays with the old insurance carrier.
    2. If the waiver is not renewed because medical information is not provided to the old insurance carrier during the waiver renewal period,[a] the Insured's Group Interest will terminate.
    3. Terminated Master Policies usually provide for a conversion option.
       A. Conversion options generally have a maximum death benefit cap of $2,000.00 to $10,000.
    4. To be eligible for the conversion option, generally an Insured must have been covered for at least five (5) years to be eligible.
    5. Conversion would result in significantly less death benefit for ABC than the amount acquired.

E. **Reduced Coverage Due to Change of Salary of Insured**
    1. Some group polices provide for increased or decreased insurance based on the salary of the Insured. Thus, if the Insured's salary is reduced, coverage will decline.
    2. ABC shall only acquire Group Interests

---

[a] Usually a three month period.

where coverage is frozen.

3. However, there still is a risk that if the Insured is on disability and returns to work part time at a lower salary, coverage could be reduced. This is most likely to occur if the Employer changed insurance carriers during the time ABC holds the Group Interest.

F. **Change of Insurance Coverage While Insured is Working**

1. In the event the Employer changes insurance carriers, risks are greater than with an Insured who is on disability premium waiver.

2. With an Insured who is not on disability premium waiver, the old Group Interest will disappear when the Employer acquires a new Master Policy.

3. ABC will only acquire group interests from Insureds who are on a disability premium waiver.

G. **Termination of Group Policy Upon Age 65**

1. Most group policies terminate or reduce coverage when the Insured reaches age 65.

2. ABC will not acquire any Group Interest which terminates within 15 years of the date of acquisition due to the age of the Insured.

Viatical Companies

KEY: **PC**=Parent company   **Y**=Year founded   **PR**=Principal
    L=Location   **T**=Toll free number   **LIR**= Lowest insurer rating
MPP=Min. purchase price   **St**=State licenses (funding co.)   **W**=Web site

ALI Viatical Funding (Ltd Part.)	AMG
PC= Affirmative Lifestyles Y=89 PR= P & T Wallace/James Karlak L= San Antonio, TX T= (800) 876-2991 LIR= ?? MPP= $200,000 St= Securities exemptions applied for in CA, CO, CT, FL, IL, NY W= www.aliviatical.com	PC= Neuma Y=91 PR= David-Irwin Binter L= Skokie, IL; San Fr, CA T= (800) 457-7828 LIR= A- MPP= $10,000 St= CA, NY, VT, IL, TX, OR W= N/A
Dedicated Resources	**LifeLine**
PC= Dedicated Resources Y=89 PR= Michael D. Zadoff L= Del Ray Beach, FL T= (800) 677-5026 LIR= A MPP= $20,000 St= CA, FL, TX, NY W= www.dir.com/dedresrc.html	PC= Page & Associates Y=89 PR= Scott Page L= Ft. Lauderdale, FL T= (800) 572-4346 LIR= B+ MPP= $20,000 St= CA, FL, TX, NY W= www.thelifeline.com
Legacy Capital	**Viatical Benefactors**
PC=Legacy Benefits Y=91 PR= Meir Eliav L= New York, NY T= (800) 875-1000 LIR= A MPP=$20,000 St= NY, WA, CA, OR, TX W= www.legacybenefit.com	PC= Independent Benefits Y=92 PR= R. Vincente/Aaron Kokol L= Greensboro, NC T= (800) 800-3264 LIR= A- MPP= $5,000 St= TX, CA, NY, FL W= www.ibenefit.com

Insurers and Viatication

Carole Fiedler [a]

T HE VIATICAL INDUSTRY IS FACED WITH VARIOUS CHALLENGES from large insurers. These make viatication more difficult for viators and more expensive for investors. The major challenges are fees for verification of coverage (VOC) and restrictions on assignment.

FEES FOR VERIFICATION OF COVERAGE (VOC)

Some time ago, when asked to provide VOC for an insured who wished to viaticate his life insurance, UNUM imposed a charge of $250. The Insurance Commissioner became involved in this case, and in January 1997 UNUM agreed to discontinue this charge.

Now it's Aetna's turn. On November 14, 1997, Aetna US Healthcare replied to a request for VOC with this notice:

> Effective 1/1/97 all Viatical Questionnaires will be subject to a $600.00 surcharge. Said $600.00 must be payable to Aetna US Healthcare prior to completion of the Verification of Coverage forms.

Aetna claims to provide a one-page standardized form at no charge. The form submitted by Fiedler Financial is four pages long. Obviously, these four pages request more information than Aetna willingly provides, but this information is necessary to the due diligence aspects of viatication.

Derek Gordon, a spokesman for the San Francisco AIDS Foundation said, "I can't imagine given our computer age that providing verification of

---

[a] The author, Carole Fiedler, is a viatical broker. See contributors, page 6.

coverage is a $600 expense for a company like Aetna." [a]

Whatever the reasoning behind these new charges, the practice is unethical. Instead of providing information at an insured's request, which should be a policy service, companies institute a steep charge that will put some viators at a disadvantage. If the cost to viaticate small policies is excessive, viatical funding firms may restrict purchases to policies with larger face amounts. Yet it's usually the person with the small death benefit who is in greater financial need than one who has a large policy.

It's difficult to understand why insurers such as Aetna choose to do this. Could it be the potential profit? If the viator applies to several funding firms and a broker, it's possible that an insurer will get six requests for VOC. Six requests at $600 each is not petty change.

Evidence supports this theory. According to Aetna US Healthcare spokesman Bob Pena, the company

> started charging a fee because of the growth in the number of requests for verification of coverage and the extra work required to complete them.[b]

RESTRICTIONS ON ASSIGNMENT (TRANSFER)

This provision is not new and certainly wasn't designed to thwart viatical settlements, but it serves to do just that. Many group policies allow assignments (transfer) only as a gift. That means a policy cannot be assigned for value (sold) unless the insurer grants an exception.

Over the years many insurers, upon request, have granted an exception to viators and granted them the right to an absolute assignment or assignment for value. Yet there are insurers who refuse to do this. They refuse despite the fact that the employer, who is the group policy holder, requests this exception for terminally ill employees.

---

[a] Laura Castaneda,"Aetna Catches Flax Over Verification Fee Viatical Industry." *San Francisco Chronicle,* November 24, 1997.

[b] *Ibid.*

Some relief is coming. On January 1, 1998, California ushered in AB 489. This law closed a loophole in insurance law by allowing people with terminal illnesses the same rights to viaticate group policies as those who have private insurance.

AB 489 was sponsored by AIDS Project Los Angeles (APLA), and I am proud to have played an integral role in getting it passed. The bill was opposed by the Association of California Life and Health Insurance Companies. The association argued that this provision would increase administrative costs for insurers and employers. They also claimed that their contractual obligation was to group policy holders, not to the individual insureds.

CONCLUSION

Unless a policy lapses for non-payment of premiums, insurers are required to pay death benefits. One explanation for their lack of cooperation may be that they want to ensure that premiums do not get paid and policies do lapse. Otherwise, it is beyond my comprehension why insurers repeatedly put obstacles in the paths of dying people who need cash for their final days.

ANTI-FRAUD INTERNET RESOURCES

National Association of Securities Dealers: www.investor.nasd.com

National Association of Securities Administrators
www.nasaa.org/investoredu/investoralerts/bogusira.html

Investor Protection information site: www.investorprotection.com

Securities and Exchange Commission (several items)
www.sec.gov/consumer/askqinv.htm; and: /consumer/invest2.ht

About Fraud, Investments, scams and swindles
http://www.fraud.org/
http://www.investoralert.com/iarc1.html
gopher://gopher.gsa.gov/00/staff/pa/cic/money/investor.txt
gopher://gopher.gsa.gov/00/staff/pa/cic/money/swindles.txt

"101 Questions to Ask Before Investing" is available at the state of Missouri site:
http://mosl.sos.state.mo/sos-sec/101.que.html.

About online investment schemes and scams:
            http://freenet.buffalo.edu/business/invest.schemes.html
            http://www.pueblo.gsa.gov/press/online.htm
            http://www.fraud.org/nfic2.htm

Free legal advice: http://www.freeadvice.com

State securities administrators list, with addresses, phone, fax, email at
http://www.seclaw.com/stcomm.htm

Maverick Viatical Companies:
Investors Beware

Per Larson[a]

MAVERICK COMPANIES TRADE HIGH RISK FOR HIGH RETURNS. They act as middlemen, and they don't get paid unless they make the deal. That's why they tend to make extraordinarily high offers—sometimes 15 to 25 percent more than industry norms—especially for policies held by people with relatively long life expectancies. How can this be?

When life expectancy predictions are ambiguous, these companies claim to their investors that life expectancy is really much lower. This, in turn, justifies the higher price used to attract the policy and pay broker fees.

A CAP ON HIGH OFFERS

Because mavericks pay at least three commissions—to find the buyer, find the seller, and make the deal—they often can't pay viators more than 70 to 75 percent for policies, even when the seller truly has a very low life expectancy. This means that a person in poor health is severely penalized in the maverick market while the person who sells policies speculatively makes a fortune. The result is that the market has moved from one of 60 to 85 percent offers to one of 30 to 75 percent offers, a truly ironic financial development spawned by the new AIDS drugs.

MORE WILD CARD OFFERS

Conservative firms hire several specialized doctors to evaluate cases, but in maverick firms entrepreneurs make the decisions and their offers are driven

---

[a] This article was adapted from one originally written for terminally ill sellers. For more information about Mr. Larson, see the contributors section at the beginning of the book.

as much by funds availability as by life expectancy. If the company has just received an influx of funds, offers will be abnormally high; if not, it may not be interested in bidding.

Mavericks are motivated by market competition as well. If they don't get the policy, they don't get their dealer fees and they don't hold the risk.

PRICE DIFFERENCES
Here are two cases that illustrate the sharply contrasting differences these current conditions have produced:

- A person with a high (240) T-cell count, whose life expectancy on paper was 2 to 4 years, received an offer of 63 percent from a maverick company
- A person with 10 T-cells, who had to be taken off the new drugs, received offers of 64.5 percent and 65 percent from two conservative companies.

HIDDEN TAX DANGERS
The problem is that most maverick dealers are not licensed in the key states where many people with HIV live: New York, Florida, Texas, California, and Illinois. These states require licensing. If their residents sell their life insurance to non-licensed firms, the money is taxable.

The IRS is now designing the 1099 forms by which viatical settlements paid to viators will be declared in January of each year. As yet, there is no procedure for the buyers (investors). Nor is there any clue as to what information will be asked of buyers. This lack of definition sets the stage for misinterpretation, lost information, and exploitation by the unscrupulous.

In their eagerness to seal a deal, some brokers and dealers use this delay to either downplay or deny the taxability of these sales or these requirements. Yet federal law is absolutely clear on this point.

DECEPTIVE SALES PRACTICES
Many brokers falsely claim that if they are licensed in the state of the seller, all's well. This is patently untrue.

Then there are the residency games played by some viatical companies. They change residency to states that don't license viatical firms. However, IRS residency requirements are very strict—and the state of residency is not easily changed. Consult an attorney if you have any doubts about a company's state of residency.

TAX FALLOUT: FEWER BUYERS

Sellers in states that require licensing have far fewer buyers to choose from. Many conservative firms have ceased operations; most maverick firms are not licensed.

In New York, for example, there are only a few conservative and maverick firms left. In California a similar dramatic fall has taken place. Illinois had only five licensed firms for a year after it started licensing; now it has seven.

This lack of legitimate players restricts competitive bidding and bars people in states that license firms from getting tax-free settlements from the maverick firms currently making extraordinary mid-range offers.

FEWER SAFEGUARDS

Conservative firms sought state licensing as a way to standardize industry practice and give sellers credibility and confidence in buyers. Maverick firms often don't qualify by state licensing standards—or don't want strict overview of their operations. This produces some dangers for sellers:

- Unlicensed firms do not pay money into a genuine escrow account held by a truly independent attorney.
- Commissions, bonuses, and secret side agreements with brokers are almost never disclosed.
- Contracts are not subject to the review of any regulatory agency.
- The contract page dealing with price can be changed unless buyers initial each page.

WOLVES IN SHEEP'S CLOTHING

Maverick dealers increasingly have their own captive brokers. A captive broker appears to offer brokering to many buyers but in fact, funnels sellers to only one company. One conservative firm uses insurance agents to funnel clients in a similar way.

OFFER PATTERNS

Maverick companies are far more naive in medical analysis than conservative firms because they're using other people's money and their offers are market driven or funds driven rather than based on strict technical analysis.

Most mavericks still talk in terms of T-cell counts; few seem to rely on viral-load measures. An analysis of offers this year shows no correlation with viral-load and the amount of viatical settlement. Statistical analysis of one set of offers made throughout 1977 shows that T-cell count still is a good rough indicator of likely offer range:

♦ Where T-counts were less than 50, offers were all in the mid-70 percent range.

♦ Where T-counts were 100 to 150, offers were in the 60 percent range. However, great variation begins to be seen. Here are examples of four offers in the 100 to 125 T-count range: 55 percent, 60 percent, 69 percent, and 70 percent! Examples of other offers where the T-count was 150 were 57 percent, 60 percent, and 66 percent.

♦ Where T-counts were over 200, offers fell to the 50 percent range—but there was an offer for 59 percent where the T-count was 250.

♦ Where T-counts were 300, offers fell to the 40 percent range—but the statistics ranged from 37 to 50 percent.

♦ Some offers of over 30 percent have occurred in the low-400 T-count range.

SHORT-TERM UNCERTAINTIES

♦ If articles are written about the scandal of small investors being defrauded, offers may fall.

♦ If more and more investors find they own policies on very healthy people, some mavericks may go out of business.

♦ Class action suits against some mavericks are being readied.

♦ Hard research reveals that the volume of the largest maverick firm has fallen by over 85 percent. As this firm's funds became scarce, its offers went down.

♦ If the stock market falls , investors may become cautious.

If the market implodes because of these factors, is this the end of viatication? Not likely. This innovation is here to stay, although dramatic changes will continue. Like it or not, viatication is a lifesaver for many in desperate circumstances.

LONG-TERM OPTIMISM

Americans seem willing to invest in anything in the current market. Since small investor funds are usually "pooled" to buy a policy, these investors have little ability to investigate or monitor the facts. Small investors left owning shares in the policies may not know the deal was bad until 2 to 4 years later.

Moreover, it's easy for a company to recruit funds and set up as a maverick again. In the longer run, as it becomes easier for conservative companies to predict how patients may react to the new drugs, a new viatical market will emerge—one based more on technical analysis than on market or financial factors. Mid-range speculative offers may fall but offers for those in poor health may rise.

Expect more states to require licensing. At first licensing will restrict the number of bidders for a tax-free settlement. But states with strict licensing like New York are rewriting their statutes to accommodate and regulate the mavericks. As this happens this market will stabilize.

State Securities Regulation

Sales of fractionalized shares of viatical contracts are considered securities in an increasing number of states. Under this definition viatical contracts may not be sold unless the investment is registered with the state agency that regulates securities and the sale is conducted by registered representatives—people licensed by those states to sell securities within its borders. When an entity is found to violate these laws, the first legal remedy usually is an order to "cease and desist" those activities.[a]

Cease and Desist Orders issued by Missouri against unregistered companies and the individuals who sold these investments demonstrate several points made throughout the text.[b] In the first example Aide the Living, Inc. (ATL), a Michigan-based viatical company, was not registered with the Missouri state securities department, nor was the viatical investment or the sales agents. In addition, ATL was charged with failing to disclose pertinent medical information, misrepresenting material facts, and fraudulent practices.[c] These charges were based on items supplied to investors by ATL:

- Correspondence purportedly to an investor in a viatical settlement contract advising of the death of the viator. This correspondence projected rates of return that ranged from 44.44 to 66.67 percent, (depending on whether death occurred as late as 90 days after investing or as soon as 60 days after investing).
- A copy of a facsimile presented as sales material to the investor, from

---

[a] "Cease and Desist" are legal terms to order a person or business to stop operating. Penalties usually are slight, if any.

[b] As in the original documents, the viator's confidentiality is protected by referring to him as "V1," and the identity of the Missouri resident is protected by referring to him/her as "MR."

[c] The principals of Aide the Living were Clare W. Willman and Scott Willman.

a party named "Deborah" to S. Willman which reads as follows:[a]

> URGENT! URGENT! Please call me about Dale . . . . He is having his power shut off Wednesday. Can we wire $1,000 Tuesday and the balance Wednesday? Please say "yes." Call me.

♦ An undated list of 19 matured ATL policies. Only one policy went beyond the estimated life expectancy (by 3 months), 14 policies matured prior to the shortest life expectancy estimate, and the remaining four were within the life expectancy range. The list also showed an average annual return of 40.65 percent.

♦ A document entitled, "Commonly Asked Questions About Viatical Settlements." This document misrepresented material facts including that the life expectancy of AIDS patients could be reasonably predicted, and that newly developed drug treatments had an insignificant potential effect on life expectancies of AIDS patients.

♦ This document also described how the insured's medical condition was confirmed—using 3 sources:

1. The Viator must complete an extensive questionnaire about his medical history. He must also authorize the release of all medical records including the records of the attending physician, hospital records and laboratory reports.

2. The attending physician must provide a thorough medical record of the patient providing detailed information on the progress of the patient's condition, treatments and prognosis. He must also certify the insured's mental competency.

3. An independent reviewing physician must examine all relevant medical records and concur with the attending physician's prognosis. Further, the reviewing physician must independently estimate the insured's life expectancy. It is this anticipated life expectancy that is used by ATL to evaluate the anticipate term of the policy holding period.

---

[a] Willman is one of ATL's principals.

♦ The following medical report which summarized the condition of the insured ("V1") was given to the investor:

Applicant is a 30 year old male diagnosed HIV positive, with full blown AIDS in 1992. T-cell count was 160 as of December, 1995. Patient has displayed an intolerance to all anti-viral treatments to date. Opportunistic infections include herpes simplex, condiolymata acuminata, anemia, and wasting syndrome. Patient also has had indications of . . . fatigue, night sweats, fever, and chills. The early onset of opportunistic infections, low and falling T-cell count, intolerance for anti-viral treatments, and chronic symptoms suggests a mid term potential for crisis. ATL physician predicts life expectancy of 18 to 30 months.

♦ At a later date ATL sent letters to investors informing them that it was necessary to sell the AIDS policies now, due to the effect of protease inhibitors on life expectancy. If they held on to these policies, they might become "unsalable."[a]

♦ ATL was the owner of these policies—not the investor. In preparation for the sale, ATL planned to get updated life expectancies to determine sales prices. ATL hired viatical broker Deborah Rhoades of Viatical Clearing House, and asked her to arrange for new life expectancy estimates.

♦ Rhoades contracted with American Viatical Services for new life expectancy estimates on these policies.

♦ A "Mortality Profile" dated November 19, 1997, prepared by American Viatical Services, described the same patient:

American Viatical Services has reviewed in detail the medical records forwarded to our company on . . . by Viatical Clearing

---

[a] This contradicted earlier messages from ATL which discounted the possibility of any therapy being developed and approved for use within the foreseeable future.

> House, including attending physician's medical records, laboratory records and radiology reports. . . . We have discussed his medical records with his personal physician. V1 is a 31-year-old male . . . The past medical history for V1 is significant for no opportunistic infections or constitutional symptoms. He is asymptomatic at this time. No weight history is available. . . . V1's prognosis is good to fair due to the absence of opportunistic infections, T-cell values above 500 . . . . The projected mortality for V1 is 48 to 60 months.

Additionally, American Viatical Services had a discussion with V1's physician and concluded:

> The physician confirms that V1 is not compliant with office visits . . . but has had little progression of the disease for several years.

Compare the medical summary given to investors by ATL with the evaluation prepared by American Viatical Services. Is it possible that there are two viators with the same name, same social security number, same insurance policy, but radically different medical histories?

In another action, Missouri issued Cease and Desist Orders against Capwill and Company, James A. Capwill, C.P.A., Portfolio Liquidation Services (PLS), Liberte Capital Group, and J. Richard Jamieson. According to the Cease and Desist Orders, these entities made an offer to purchase the viatical settlement contract interests of a Missouri investor.

This situation is different in that the investor initially purchased his shares from Alabama-based Life Options International (LOI).[a] The parties named in the Cease and Desist told the investor that if he did not resell his interests to them, he would be responsible for premium payments on the underlying life insurance policies. The most significant issues are as follows:

♦ The investor was told at the time of purchase that the purchase price was complete and inclusive, and if premiums had to be paid at some future date Life Options would pay them. In other words, the investor was told he would not have any further expenses.

---

[a] This company no longer exists.

♦ In April 1996 Life Options sold its assets and transferred its service liabilities to Ohio-based Viatical Solutions, Inc. (VSI). VSI then engaged Viatical Escrow Services, of which James Capwill, CPA, is managing director, to act as escrow agent.

♦ In December 1997 Liberte executed a Letter of Intent to purchase the "life insurance portfolio" held by VSI. The portfolio included the policies in which the Missouri investor "owned" shares.

♦ Portfolio Liquidators hired James Capwill to liquidate the portfolios previously owned by VSI and Life Options.

♦ A letter sent to investors informed them that Portfolio Liquidators had secured the rights to liquidate certain viatical settlement contracts that remained unmatured past life expectancy.

♦ Investors were informed that if they chose not to sell, they would have to pay "significant dollars" or "confront the dire reality of total worthlessness. . . ."

♦ An investigator with Missouri Division of Securities learned that PLS was an entity "set up by Rick Jamieson and Liberte Capital Group."[a]

♦ In March 1998 the Missouri Division of Securities received information that indicated that VSI had not sold its viatical settlement contract portfolio to PLS.

♦ When Missouri officials attempted to get further information from the parties, their inquiries met with no response. Capwill said that he did not have access to the information and did not have time to respond to the request.

♦ Missouri's Division of Securities determined omissions of material facts in connection with the offer and sale of securities constitute fraudulent and thus illegal practices under the statute.

♦ Misrepresentations of material facts in connection with the offer and sale of securities constitute fraudulent and thus illegal practices under the statute.

---

[a] Liberte is the company that wanted to buy this portfolio.

Among the material facts that were misrepresented:

1. That Portfolio Liquidation Services secured the rights to liquidate certain viatical contracts that had previously been owned by or serviced by either VSI or LOI.

2. That investors were not told their shares could be sold for less than the investment.

3. That investors were assured they would not have to pay premiums.

The Cease and Desist Order does not reveal if investors were informed at the time of purchase that ownership of the policy would be vested in the viatical company.

These examples should convince investors and investment advisors of the necessity of having an attorney peruse any viatical investment contract they are considering. If the language of the contract is obtuse, also ask the attorney to prepare a plain English interpretation. The cost for this service will be less than one percent of the investment that may be at risk.

Viatical Investment Checklist

1. Determine if this is the right investment for you.
2. Avoid buying through sales agents or marketing companies.
3. Check with your state securities department to find out if viatical investments are considered securities.
4. Make purchases through financial professionals who are licensed to sell other investment products, who have a duty to perform due diligence for investments they recommend, *and* who deal directly with viatical funding firms.
5. Check the credentials (including complaint history) of the stockbroker or insurance agent who offers this investment. Check with NASD and/or the state department of insurance.
6. Insist on policies that were purchased by companies that meet the *criteria* listed in chapter 4, "Contracts Compared."
7. Beware of life insurance policies that are within the contestability period.
8. Beware of policies that may have been issued fraudulently.
9. Beware of policies that may have been issued in violation of local law.
10. Get resumes for all medical experts. Ask about the method(s) they use to predict life expectancy.
11. Be certain you (and co-owners, if applicable) are listed as owners.
12. Be certain you (and co-owners, if applicable) are listed as irrevocable beneficiary(ies).
13. Be certain the escrow account is held in a federally chartered bank.
14. Enlist an attorney with expertise in securities to review the contract.
15. If the contract doesn't spell out all terms, conditions, and fees, insist that missing information be added and signed by a principal of the company who has authority to do so.
16. Try to arrange to pay premium and tracking fees as they come due, rather than in advance at the time of closing. This assures that a company that becomes financially strained doesn't use these essential funds for administrative purposes and neglect premiums or tracking fees.
17. Don't use IRA savings for viatical investments until there is a definitive decision by the Internal Revenue Service or the courts.
18. Plan to pay taxes on the gain.
19. Don't place all your eggs in the viatical basket.

GLOSSARY

Ab initio— From the beginning

Absolute Assignment— The transfer of ownership rights

Accelerated Death Benefits — Pre-death benefits paid by an insurance carrier

Assignable— Permits transfer to another party

Assignee—The entity (e.g., person; company) to whom a policy is assigned

Association insurance— Insurance for groups with a common interest

Beneficiary— The person named to receive the death benefits

Broker— A viatical provider who assists viators with finding a buyer and negotiating a price

Cash out—To cancel an insurance policy in exchange for its net cash surrender value

Contestability period— The two year period in which an insurance contract can be canceled for cause by an insurer

Convert—Transfer from group to individual ownership, or from term to permanent insurance

Closing— The time when money and the life insurance policy are formally exchanged, similar to "closing" of escrow on real estate; transfer

Conversion cap— The maximum face amount allowed for a group policy converted to an individual policy

Death benefit—The amount paid to a beneficiary. Also known as face valueor face amount

Decreasing term—Term insurance in which the death benefit reduces over time (e.g., mortgage insurance)

Disability waiver— A rider that excuses premium payments when an insured has been disabled for longer than six months

Escrow—A temporary holding account for funds

Evidence of Insurability— Information about health, occupation, lifestyle, habits, income, net worth and other insurance

FEGLI—Federal Employees Government Life Insurance

Flexible premium adjustable life—Universal Life Insurance

Fractionalized shares— Percentages of a life insurance policy for sale; co-ownership

Funding sources—Direct buyers of life insurance death benefits. Also known as funding firms or capitalization firms

Grace period—Time period for an insured to change his/her mind

Graded life—Life insurance for people with serious health conditions; pays lower benefits in early years if death is from sickness

Guaranteed Insurability Option (GIO)—The right to increase the death benefit without evidence of Insurability

Guaranteed issue life—See graded life

Incontestability clause— Prohibits an insurer from canceling a life or disability contract except for failure to pay premiums

INDs—Investigational New Drugs

Irrevocable—Cannot be changed

Insurable Interest—The beneficiary suffers loss when an insured dies

Lapse—Cease to be in force

Legal competency—Of sound mind

Maturity—The date when death benefits are payable, due to the demise of the insured

Maverick—Unlicensed viatical companies

Ordinary life—Permanent, whole life (cash value) insurance

Policy loan—Funds borrowed from the cash value of a life insurance company

Policy holder—The owner of an insurance policy

Premium—Payment required to keep a policy in force

Rating—Extra charge for an insured who is greater than standard insurance risk

Reinstate— To put a policy put back in force after it lapsed

Rescind—Cancel

Rider—A provision in an insurance contract that changes the benefits

SGLI—Servicemen's/women's Government Life Insurance

Term insurance— Life insurance without cash value. Premiums increase upon renewal

Tracking—The process of monitoring the viator until death

Transfer for value—Money is exchanged

Underwriting—The process of evaluating financial risk

Universal Life—A cash value policy that combines term insurance and an investment. Also known as Flexible Premium Adjustable Life

Variable Life—Similar to Universal Life Insurance except that the policy-holder determines where the savings portion is invested

VGLI—Veteran's Government Life Insurance

Viatical settlement—Payment made in exchange for beneficiary rights to a life insurance policy

Viaticate—To sell a life insurance policy

Viaticum— A viatical settlement

Viator—The insured who contracts to sell a life insurance policy

Waive— To excuse, as premiums or tax penalties

Waiver of premium— Premium payments are excused by an insurer when an insured has been totally disabled for six months

Whole life—Cash value, permanent life insurance, usually with level premiums payable for the term of the policy (e.g., to age 65 or for life)

INDEX

Fractionalized shares, 34, 146, 184, 211

Fraud, 25, 31, 91, 105, 107, 117, 118, 129, 137, 140, 142, 157, 160, 161, 163, 173, 212, 217

G

Group policies, 50, 193, 197

Guarantees, 38, 39, 91, 92, 121, 159, 161

H

Hasty, Marian L., 175

I

Illegal sale, 147

Imposter, 49, 138-139, 141, 160, 162

Incontestability, 138-140 , 143, 158, 159, 160, 162

IND's, 111, 114

Insurance, 47-48, 93, 101

Insurers, 35, 36, 101, 122, 160, 162

Internet, 46, 130, 201

Investigational new drugs
see, INDs

IRA, 31, 32, 92, 174, 176-178

IRS, 31, 32, 206

J

Joint and several liability, 84

L

Legacy Capital, 65, 69, 71, 72, 74, 75, 77-80, 82, 86, 87, 91, 98, 99, 104

Legal competency, 92

Liability release, 49

Liberte Capital Group, 215

License, 32-34, 65

Life expectancy, 39, 50, 52, 58, 72, 79, 86, 92, 109, 111-117, 163, 182, 205, 206, 213

Life insurance, 103-105, 145

Life Options, 216

Life Partners, 24, 32, 35, 53, 68, 65, 95, 176, 183, 146

LifeLine, 65, 70-72, 74, 75, 79, 78, 83, 85, 87, 89, 90, 99, 168

Liquidity, 90, 170

Loans
IRA, 32
policy, 53, 82, 83

Loy, Phil, 55, 96

M

Master policy, 194, 195

Material misrepresentation,

About the Author

A NATIONALLY RECOGNIZED AUTHORITY ON VIATICAL settlements, Gloria Grening Wolk is author of *Cash for the Final Days: A Financial Guide for the Terminally Ill and their Advisors*, the first published book about viatical settlements.

Ms. Wolk began her career in financial services in 1984, as an award-winning career agent with the Norwalk, Connecticut office of Lincoln National Corporation, one of the nation's largest diversified financial institutions. In addition to earning a Certificate in Financial Planning from The American College, she attended numerous seminars on estate planning, employee benefits, and taxation.

After relocating to California in 1990, Ms. Wolk began to specialize in disability financial planning. Although she continues to hold licenses for life, health, and disability insurance and is a licensed tax preparer, Ms. Wolk concentrates her time and energies on creating articles and books as well as offering seminars and consulting services.

A proud graduate of CCNY and the University of Connecticut Graduate School of Social Work, Gloria Wolk lives near the Pacific Ocean in Orange county, California, with her German Shepherds, Ninja and Trudy. She can be reached by email at: <GGWOLK@viatical-expert.net>.

Note: Bialkin Books sponsors a Web site on the Internet with continuously up-dated information on Viatical Settlements based on research by the author.

To view this site, go to **http://www.viatical-expert.net**.